# Saint Croix Notes

W9-CGX-464

# Saint Croix Notes

NOAH ADAMS

Houghton Mifflin Company • Boston

For information about permission to reproduce selections
from this book, write to W. W. Norton & Company, Inc.,
500 Fifth Avenue, New York, New York 10110.

Since this page cannot legibly accommodate all the
copyright notices, page 221 constitutes an extension
of the copyright page.

*Library of Congress Cataloging-in-Publication Data*
Adams, Noah
  Saint Croix notes / Noah Adams.
      p.      cm.
   ISBN 0-395-59704-8
   1. Saint Croix notes (Radio program)   I. Title.
PN1991.77.S25A36   1992   91-20010   CIP
791.44'72—dc20
Printed in the United States of America

Book design by Guenet Abraham.

HAD 10 9 8 7 6 5 4 3 2 1

Houghton Mifflin Company paperback, 1991

I n the 1950s in Ashland, Kentucky, in a white frame house five blocks up the hill from the main street, in my grandfather's room, there was a radio. A brown Bakelite RCA Victor table model. The dial was always lit. After school and after supper, I was my grandfather's radio-listening buddy. "The Lone Ranger," "One Man's Family," "The Fat Man" . . . the weather and the news and the baseball games. He would go to sleep with the radio on; he had little use for the new television out in the living room.

My grandfather had retired early, and stayed busy. He kept a daily journal, he always had letters to write, he saved articles from the newspapers, and he filled empty cigar boxes with clippings and rubber bands, and string and stamps and paper clips (he'd quit smoking but usually had an unlit cigar in his mouth, for the taste of the tobacco). He spent most of his time sitting in an old oak Morris chair, with his pencils and notes and scissors and cellophane tape spread out on a lapboard. There was a shiny black Smith and Corona on top of a dresser, and he stood up to type, his head tilted back to see through his bifocals. And then, with a stack of envelopes, he would try to find someone to drive him downtown. He didn't trust the corner mailbox; his letters had to go in the brass slots in the lobby of the main post office.

My grandfather also shared my delight in sending away for things we'd heard about on the radio. We'd tape a quarter to a piece of cardboard, or collect three cereal box tops, and then wait the long weeks for a badge or a decoder ring. And I can remember trying to learn to tap dance in his room. Some big-band music would be on the radio from Chicago. He would put the lapboard from the chair down on the carpet, and I would hold myself up with my arms, pushing from his bed and the side of a table—and dance. He'd keep time with a pencil, and laugh.

Years later when I took my first job in radio, after college hadn't worked out, he became fond of rock and roll music, staying up late to listen. His grandson was on the radio, and he must have been smiling and proud.

I was pretty pleased myself. Five nights a week playing rock and roll, talking on the phone, reading dedications.

"Please play 'Roses Are Red, Violets Are Blue,' by Bobby Vinton, for Rick and Susie, Tommy and Jo Ann, Larry and Janet P. . . ."

I also went out to the junior high schools in the afternoons to emcee "Coca-Cola Sock Hops." And the local drive-in movie asked me to make an intermission tape to be played on the car speakers, between movies. I would put together the week's top five songs, a musical countdown, along with commercials for the concession stand. Then on Saturday night I'd take a date to the movie, wait for intermission, and . . . *my* voice on the speaker, echoing across the gravel parking lot, my voice, making jokes, pushing the hot dogs and popcorn, talking about the first four songs, and I was the only one who knew what the number one record was going to be!

When I would sign the radio station off at midnight, "WIRO now comes to the end of another broadcasting day . . . ," I'd drive home listening to the great fifty-thousand-watt stations—WLS in Chicago. Clark Weber would play the same music I played, and I thought for the first few months that I was as good as he was. We were both big-time rock and roll deejays. But then I started making air-check tapes of my shows and paying closer attention to the announcers on the clear-channel stations, and I began to understand that I was simply a beginner.

My most humbling moment on radio came some twenty-five years later, in 1976. That year all the Nobel Prize winners were Americans, and I was sent to Sweden to broadcast the award ceremonies. During a very solemn moment in Stockholm's Town Hall, when the economist Milton

Friedman was accepting his award from the king of Sweden, a man ran into the auditorium blowing a whistle and yelling quite loudly, obviously in protest. I said to the listeners in the United States, "He's yelling something in a foreign language." Our translator, sitting next to me and helping with the broadcast, said calmly, "No, Noah, he's yelling in Swedish."

My second career in broadcasting began in 1972. My rock and roll years hadn't lasted very long, and by the early seventies I was doing construction work, writing some free-lance advertising copy, trying to settle on a career. National Public Radio had begun operations. "All Things Considered" was on the air; it sounded brand-new and important. And late one night I heard a program called "Sound on Film," which featured a conversation with James Dickey. "Sound on Film," as I learned later, was produced in Hollywood and sent out free to radio stations, as a way to promote new films.

James Dickey was talking about the movie *Deliverance*. He had written the screenplay from his own novel. I had seen the film already and read the book, but Dickey's description that night, the story of his hero's climb up a dangerous and dark cliff out in the wilds of Georgia, escaping the killers, was vivid and frightening. The radio version of this scene, as told in the author's soft accent, seemed more compelling than the movie or book had been. And I began to understand that radio, done well, would be worth a try.

I volunteered to work for the local public station, again as a deejay, playing progressive rock music on a show called "After Midnight" and bluegrass music on "Kentucky

Blue." I played classical music as well, even though I didn't know much about it (people would call up after I had tried to pronounce a composer's name and say, "Nice try"). After I joined the staff full-time, I produced a news documentary, and helped train students who were thinking about broadcasting as a career, although many of them just wanted help in getting rid of their Appalachian accents. In the fall of 1975 I moved to Washington to work for National Public Radio as a tape editor and writer. I was thirty-three then, and the producer told me later he had wanted someone a little older, someone who knew who Solzhenitsyn was. I nodded wisely, as if I had actually read Solzhenitsyn.

Twelve years later, when an offer came to go out to Saint Paul and develop a new radio program that would follow Garrison Keillor's "A Prairie Home Companion," the chance to try something else for a time was welcome. I had done hundreds of stories for "All Things Considered" and thousands of interviews. I was feeling a bit caught up in the news, and I thought often about some lines from a William Carlos Williams poem:

> *It is difficult*
> *to get the news from poems*
> *yet men die miserably every day*
> *for lack*
> *of what is to be found there.*

I was also intrigued by the fantastic notion of doing a radio program on a stage in front of people. My response, when I thought of it, was almost physical—a quick intake of breath and a shudder, like the sense of falling that you can suddenly have crossing a high bridge. I've always had stage fright, could hardly face an audience, even just to answer questions from a group of public radio listeners. How can *he* be scared, they would ask themselves, he's on the radio every night. How *can* I be scared, I would say to myself. Go try it, I thought, it will be a good experience. And there was something else, something from long ago. A thought that would come while drifting off to sleep at night. I was somehow on a stage in front of an audience, alone. And in the years to come, in moments of fantasy I'd remember that image, convinced it was a premonition, almost a calling.

The World Theater was built in Saint Paul in 1910 by the Shubert brothers, the first playhouse west of Chicago without pillars supporting the balconies. It had sixteen dressing rooms, a stage that could be raised and lowered, a built-in vacuum cleaning system, and two thousand electric lights. Seventy-five years later the World had been saved from demolition and restored; the seats were red, the balconies golden, the Wurlitzer organ was ready. The stage of the World Theater turned out to be a comfortable, reassuring place.

I asked a director from Minneapolis to come by and help me with the rudiments of stagecraft. He said, don't look at the people on the main floor, it seems as though you're looking down on them. Look out at the railing of the first balcony; then you appear to be looking at the whole theater. Glance up from time to time to the second balcony. They've paid good money to see you and they can't, hardly. Downstage is to the front, upstage to the back (in the old days stages were raked, slanted from the back to the front). Stage left, stage right? It's from the actor's perspective. Walk onstage with confidence, stand as close to the audience as you can get, don't hide behind anything. Stand with your arms open, your legs apart—it's almost sexual. If you open yourself to the audience, they will accept you. If you don't they won't. And yes, there is a power spot onstage, where actors feel more secure. Every stage is different, though, and every actor.

My own power spot proved elusive, but I have never felt more alive than in the fifteen minutes or so just before five o'clock on those Saturday evenings. The audience would be coming in, often more than nine hundred people, a large digital clock would be counting down to the start of the program, straight up at five. I'd walk around backstage, feeling both exhilarated and panicked. Our stage manager once, recognizing the look in my eyes, came up to me and said, "I could have a cab out back in a minute—you could get to the airport quick."

The time for "Saint Croix Notes" would come along about ten minutes before the end of each show. I would walk out and sit on a stool near the front of the stage and arrange my script on a music stand. The theater would be dark, the audience wonderfully quiet. And I would pause between words, and imagine the silence being heard a quarter of a second later as Wrangell, Alaska, and Presque Isle, Maine, and St. Louis, Missouri, and Athens, Ohio, received the satellite signal.

You are told, starting out in this business, that you should have a picture in your mind of one radio, one listener only.

And just talk directly to that person. Arthur Godfrey figured that out back in the early fifties. Before then, there was a lot of *announcing* on the radio. He said his program was for only one housewife, there in her kitchen. If her neighbor came over to borrow a cup of sugar, the two of them would be talking, the radio playing unheard in the background.

Last fall we spent some time in Maine, on the coast of East Penobscot Bay, in the hamlet of Harborside. My wife, Neenah, had long wanted to meet Helen Nearing, who lived nearby at Forest Farm. Helen and Scott Nearing, in the sixties, were patron saints of the back-to-the-earth movement. They had made a living from their land and by their own labor for decades, first in Vermont, then on the coastal farm in Maine.

Helen told Neenah that now she did listen to the radio quite a lot, for classical music in the mornings (she's a violinist) and the news programs, but they hadn't had a radio when Scott was alive. Scott, who could be an old rascal at times, always said of the voices on the radio, "These are people we wouldn't invite into our homes, why would we let them come in on the radio?" A fair question, I thought.

The essays that comprise *Saint Croix Notes* were written over the twelve months of 1988, usually at sunrise on Saturday mornings, to be read that evening on the radio. I would get up in the dark and make coffee and talk to the dog some and then sit at the computer and think about how the week had gone, and what I had seen and read and listened to. The weather was always important, it seemed, and the sky, and the Saint Croix River, and it was a good year, with time for adventure and investigation, and with friends—listeners—around the country waiting to hear the stories.

One evening in the World Theater, as we were ending a show, I thought of my grandfather. Everyone onstage was smiling, having a grand time singing verses to a song called "Waltzing with Bears." It's about a man who insists—every night—on going dancing with the bears. That's just the sort of nonsense my grandfather would have loved.

# Saint Croix Notes

It's overcast, almost foggy. Down in the kitchen, the cat wants in, the dog wants out. I go into the garden to gather some marigolds. They smell sweet, raspy somehow. In this light their yellows and deep reds are almost incandescent. I can understand why movie directors like to film on gray, overcast days.

I make some coffee and think about fresh apple cider. The first taste of fall. We are coming fast into good apple time. We'll try to make some jelly this year, and certainly will make applesauce—pale, golden, chunky—lots of different apples to choose from and blend. I've tasted the Beacon apple already—it's an early ripener—tart and summer fresh. There is an apple named State Fair, with harvest dates August 18th through the 25th.

We've been out to the fair twice, once early, around seven, for breakfast. We sat alongside families who came to exhibit and stay the whole time. Young boys, brothers, with clipped haircuts, having milk and sweet rolls and sausage, smiling at another day.

We walk through some of the buildings to see the bunnies, the dwarf Netherlands, and the mini-lops, looking like expensive cats. The Alpine goats are having green alfalfa for breakfast, the cows are lined up to be milked, their owners visiting and joking.

One does not in early morning go into the midway. It would be like a nightclub open to the light of day. I always wonder, though, about the folks who travel and work on the midway, who sell the tickets, who try to coax you into picking up a baseball or darts or a squirt gun. Many of us like to think that once we would have left town with the carnival that came through in the summer. Every week a different town, bright lights, music—you get to smoke a lot. There is a term in carnival lore, "twenty-milers," for those who join up, make the next stop twenty miles down the road, but then get homesick, maybe feel guilty.

We saw Chuck Berry at the fair one night, performing at the grandstand. He is sixty-two years old. The discussions about whether people can get too old to sing rock and roll don't include him because he just . . . does. Someone sitting

behind me said, "How old is Chuck getting to be now
. . . isn't he about forty-two?"

I do know that he can still make me want to dance, and
I guess we are indeed going to get on up into our fifties,
hanging on to rock and roll. Not long ago I was watching
a couple of carpenters working on a porch—older guys.
They had one of those loud radios . . . listening to "Jumpin'
Jack Flash"—the Rolling Stones song—on a radio station
that carries advertising for a local retirement village.

You have to pay attention, don't you? Sometimes life's
going by pretty fast.

I find I have to make myself notice a lot of things. I spent
a few hours Thursday in an art center in Minneapolis. I
actually spent time inside, usually I just like to go to the gift
shop. But I went in and wandered through the rooms of
light and white walls.

> — I saw a sculpture by Miró, *Standing Woman* it's
>   called. Four feet high, bronze.
> — A painting called *Forest Fire,* orange and black,
>   latex paint and tar on vinyl over Masonite. Donald
>   Sultan, the artist.
> — Andy Warhol, a silkscreen photographic montage
>   of Jacqueline Kennedy entitled *16 Jackies.*
> — Donald Judd, a stainless steel and blue Plexiglas
>   rectangular block, in the middle of the room. Unti-
>   tled.
> — An oil painting by Marsden Hartley, of a dark
>   lakeshore and trees and a small mountain. It's
>   called *Beaver Lake, Lost River Region.*

— Some Louise Nevelson sculptures—black painted wood, *Young Tree II, Young Tree Six, Young Tree Nineteen,* gifts of the artist.

There's also a new major exhibit called "Sculpture Inside Outside" that includes the work of Jin Soo Kim. And the catalog says, "Kim works with broken chairs, discarded machinery, other abandoned objects wrapped in cloth—this urban refuse assumes vigorous somewhat sinister new life in the tendril-like constructions that hang from the ceiling, writhe in space and sprout from the ground." I look at some of Kim's work in a dark room. Then I leave to find the car and drive fifteen miles to the west, out in the country where the University of Minnesota operates a landscape arboretum, nine hundred acres. I walk past the gift shop, and find a map and go out into the gardens.

It is the time of chrysanthemums and dahlias. Most of the hostas are in bloom. I have seen two or three different hosta plants before; there are three hundred varieties here.

— The porcelain berry vine is almost in blossom. Three colors of flowers in one cluster—blue, lilac, and white—the speckled texture of a robin's egg.
— There are redbud trees, and honey locust.
— There's a kitchen herb garden, a medicinal garden, and a fragrance garden, with plants that smell of lemon and cinnamon and nutmeg.
— And a cloistered medieval monk's garden, with vines of bittersweet and hops.
— A dyer's garden, maintained by a local weaver's

guild, with plants providing natural dyes: marigolds, purple coneflowers, blue morning glories,
opal basil.
— Even a Japanese garden, with a waterfall and lilies
and moss, and, it is said, every stone placed by a
landscape architect. There's a small brown baby
turtle making its way, optimistically, from the trees
to the water, a kinetic part of the design.

There are gardens in the woods too, in a way. May apples
and trilliums and wild lupines and lady's slippers on the
summer schedule. On display now are the bright red berries
of jack-in-the pulpit.

And this is where you would come to see a hillside of
hawthorn trees, or a grove of maples, or mountain ash,
lindens, poplars, or pines. All part of the permanent collection of the arboretum. To save them we must now arrange
them in order.

In the last century a writer named Richard Jeffries, thinking about the parlor of his farmhouse in England, and then
regarding the world outside, wrote:

> I felt crushed when I first saw that there was no
> chair, no table, no picture, in nature. . . . Noth-
> ing especially made for man to sit on, to write
> on, to admire—not even the colour of the but-
> tercups or the beautiful sun-gleam which had
> me spellbound glowing on the water in my
> hand in the rocky cell.
> . . . I began to see dimly how much more

grandeur, beauty and hope there is in a divine chaos. . . . each thread in this carpet goes to form the pattern; but go out into my golden mead and gather ten thousand blades of grass, and it will not destroy it.

. . . I look at the sunshine and feel . . . limitless hope and possibilities.

You can find this passage in an anthology of Richard Jeffries' work called *Landscape with Figures.*

I have another memory of my two field trips this week, perhaps an even more perplexing example of the mingling of nature and human creativity. There is a lunchroom at the art center, with a final temptation just before your tray reaches the cashier. I don't resist, I already have the perfect cup of black coffee to go with it: there on a plate, one piece left, butterscotch-banana pie with whipped cream.

10 September

47 degrees

The barometer reading 30.10 and steady

T he sun is up and gleaming red. The color comes from smoke in the air, from forest fires in the West. We've had cool nights and good days, you keep finding excuses to be outside.

There's been *some* weather, a thunderstorm flickering early one morning. And one night even a light frost. The television stations had a delightful time that evening announcing the news every fourteen minutes, promising the whole story at ten o'clock. They showed us a picture of how

to cover up your tomato plants with plastic. If I had believed
a serious frost was really coming, I would have taken my
almost ripe tomatoes into bed with me.

The tomatoes are still splendid in the garden. There is
green grass in the backyards, and lots of goldenrod. In the
country the fields are full of yellow toadflax, white and
yellow flowers that look like wild snapdragons. They are
also called *Linaria vulgaris,* or better, "butter and eggs."
And—flashing in the meadows and in the bogs—the occa-
sional prairie fire, with scarlet blossoms. Along the roads
sumac shows its dusky dark red berries, one leaf out of seven
*bright* red.

We found time for a canoe trip, just a day down the river
from the north. A few other boats were out on the water,
even though it was a chilly morning, with rain coming. But
it was Labor Day, and a last chance for many.

We drifted, mostly, moving toward a grassy, sunlit bank
and lunch—peanut butter sandwiches and cider and potato
sticks. I have this difficulty beginning in the awfully hot days
of July and August, drinking all that water and needing the
salt. I can easily convince myself that potato sticks have
medicinal value.

If you are warm and sleepy and happy on the river—in
good company and in a canoe you like and all you have to
do is get home safely in time for a nap before dinner and the
season is changing to please you, the maple trees turning on
the hillsides in the quiet—you do not want to be startled by
the blasting roar of an airplane, coming fast and low around
a bend in the river directly at you, seventy-five feet above the
water. Maybe a hundred.

It's a small plane, and it's not supposed to be here. The Saint Croix is a protected scenic river, and it's dangerous and wrong and frustrating, and all I can do is raise a hand and salute the pilot as he zooms over, while we duck.

I assume, perhaps incorrectly, that a man is flying the plane, having a great time on the river.

We keep on paddling, slowly. It does not help to remind myself that we—in our canoe—are possibly as intrusive to the fish, to the turtles, as the airplane is to us.

Three days later, a three-hour drive to the north, still watching the sky. The water, off to the east, is Lake Superior, a vast and blue presence; beyond it a low line of Wisconsin lies across the way. We've come to a ridge above the lake to look for hawks, and falcons possibly, and kestrels and eagles. It's the time of migration.

There's a dust and gravel road along the ridge, a rock outdropping, a parking area, four or five cars. As far as we can see there's water, and the north shore of Minnesota. The birds come here, flying past below and above the ridge. They won't fly over the water, so Lake Superior pushes them west and south. Hawk Ridge, above Duluth, is a migratory trap.

On one September day ten years ago, they say, you could have seen thirty-one thousand broad-winged hawks passing by, flecks of pepper in a gray sky. The birds fly together in what is called a "kettle," rising like steam on the thermals close to the ridge, circling high in the warm air, and at the top releasing from the pattern and streaming south. Only a few birds pass today, though, some sharp-shinned hawks and kestrels skipping by. And lots of blue jays, low in the brush, being careful—they are a choice prey.

There's time to talk with the folks who come to the ridge every day. Molly is here, stationed on a folding chair, clipboard and weather radio at hand. Her dog is nearby—Kate, a straight-haired golden retriever.

Also Laura, who checks in here every day and with other places along the North Shore. She reports the counting numbers on a radio bird-watching program, as a volunteer for KUMD. She recalls one dark evening, August 14th, when a watcher counted four thousand nighthawks streaming past his house near the lake. Laura's news today is of a western kingbird sighting.

And Ned is here, most years, having driven up from Virginia. Ned is someone of a type I've seen all my life, mostly outdoors, gray hair, flannel shirt, khaki pants, good boots—and a smile.

Everyone has binoculars and quick eyes, looking to the north and east. "There's one, a shin, just over the hill!" They count red-tailed hawks, northern harriers, merlins, ospreys—whatever comes by. Molly says there are more eagles now—perhaps because of the ban on DDT. I ask what bird would excite them the most, coming across the ridge?

Molly says peregrine falcon. Laura has seen twice here and would like to see again the so-called snake bird, or anhinga. She shows me a picture in the guidebook—Minnesota would be far out of its range. Ned is back in his car having coffee. He says that's the only way more birds will come, if he stops watching.

The hawks that do go past are wonderful to see, daring,

floating on the air. Flocks of cedar waxwings go by, fast, safe, as long as they stay together.

It is a dangerous and long trip the birds make, when the cold weather comes. The hawks, flying south, are especially threatened by radio and television towers, the tall ones with guy wires. The people who take care of injured raptors expect to see birds with wings that have been sheared off.

This is one of the two foremost migratory viewing sites in the country. The other is Hawk Mountain in Pennsylvania. On this ridge next week, the peak of the season, thousands of people will gather from all over, watching many more thousands of birds passing.

And then the numbers will fall off. And these three people, watching birds closely, as an avocation, conviction, will stay; chilly, content, watching the sky to the north. It's good to know someone's paying attention.

These are mornings to be up early, for the light, the chill. To see a blue and silent hot-air balloon crossing the river.

We are moving toward the divided day and night of the autumnal equinox. Fall is coming, just next week. At this season, a friend told me, you should find a tree that you can see every day—it's best in the mornings—a tree that you can watch change colors.

This year mine is a small sugar maple, bright green at the

bottom, turning red halfway up, then orange at the top, with some yellow. Watch the tree, and watch summer leaving.

We found something up in a tree, while watching the leaves this week. Hanging from a branch in a large tree just out in front of the house, a hornet's nest. It's about the size of a basketball, the color of dry leaves, whorls of browns and grays and yellows. Big, arrogant hornets swarm in and out of several large holes near the bottom.

These are bald-faced hornets, and their nest is made from different kinds of wood. They chew the wood and bring it home for building material. Of the thousands of hornets now in the nest, only the queen will survive the winter.

September can be sad—the death of the green and growing world. The dry, crackling, icy and dark times of winter not too far ahead.

I was thinking of September and Frankenstein. The new play *Frankenstein—Playing with Fire,* developed at the Guthrie Theater in Minneapolis. The production traveled last January through May to several states; you may have seen it. I saw the play this week. It's closing now at the Guthrie.

This version of the story is both frightening and charming. There are two of Dr. Frankenstein's monsters in the play, one an older version of the other. They don't have green eyes, but do have green skin, white hair, and no belly button. This is a play about death and reanimation, and love and morality, lightning and electricity, caskets and graves, ice and mirrors. One phrase I wrote down on the back of the program in the dark, one person's wish: "To pursue Nature to her hiding place."

I don't know how you feel about ghosts. For me, it seems I can forget about them for a very long time, and then all of a sudden, a question, a story someone tells at lunch, a sound at night, a glimpse of nothing but possibly a face, will shiver in my mind.

My wife and I were looking at some houses a year or so ago. A couple of them were haunted; one especially, a white Victorian house on a farm way out by itself. We liked the house, sort of, but I kept going back upstairs. There was something in the hallway. Something about the window at the end of the hall. The people who lived there wanted to move; they said it was difficult to keep the house warm.

I used to walk by a certain corner in Washington, D.C., in Georgetown, on my way home. There was always a presence waiting there. Not a fearful thing, usually, but this was about five or six blocks from the long flight of stone steps used in the movie *The Exorcist.* The priest was thrown down those steps by dark forces. I haven't seen the movie, but I know about it.

Once I went on a late-night expedition down in east Texas, in Big Thicket country. We were looking for a ghost train, four of us out in the woods in the dark. It was said you could see the lantern of the railroad conductor who was killed, the lantern light shining through the trees. And I thought I could. And it was said you could hear the train rumbling along the track. I didn't at all, but when we turned to leave, I suddenly did. We recorded the sound, a low-frequency throbbing; you can hear it on the tape on good speakers or with headphones, the low sound, and our voices whispering.

My dog, of course, has his own ghostly encounters. In our last house he didn't want to go down in the basement. And our cat twitches in her sleep and moans and is easily startled. Cats see different things. One of the reasons you have a cat, is it not, is so that a sound at night somewhere in the house can be just the cat and not something else.

Out in the Saint Croix River Valley you can hear some talk of spirits, of healers and seers. Of people who are afraid to leave their houses, of houses where no one will live. There are pioneer graveyards abandoned in the woods. Much of the valley resembles New England and the East.

It makes me think of John Gardner's novel *Mickelsson's Ghosts,* a story set in the mountains of Pennsylvania near the Susquehanna River. A divorced and drinking professor of philosophy buys an old farmhouse of "local reputation." He smells a freshly baked cake at night. There's a crash in the basement. He watches shadows peering at him like children in hiding. And he hears voices quarreling, he even knows the names of the ghosts. Gardner describes one meeting with the Spragues:

> When Mickelsson turned, slowly, as if to stir no breeze, they were standing there, perfectly still, the old woman's face bloodless gray, her eyes full of lightning. She wore a flowerprint housedress with a faded pink robe over it, her dark, graying hair brushed straight down, to the backs of her knees. . . . The old man was in stockingfeet and workworn trousers, only a washed-out gray undershirt above, white bristly

hair poking out like a hundred tentacles around the neck. . . . Mickelsson stood still as they moved past him, the two never glancing in his direction, watching the floor.

It may be a dream or a vision or real, Professor Mickelsson is never sure.

I used to be more scared of ghosts than I am now. I was reading the *New Yorker* this week, a "Talk of the Town" story about Ted Turner, the founder of the Cable News Network, and about a videotape his company has put together. The tape shows the combined armed forces' marching bands playing the hymn "Nearer, My God, to Thee." The videotape is intended to be played on CNN in the event of a nuclear attack on the United States.

There are things—certainly—more frightening than ghosts, less wonderful than Nature in her hiding place.

1 October

54 degrees

The barometer reading 29.97 and falling

A cold front, the weather radio says, is moving across the Great Plains. It's been warm and pleasant for a week or so, with a good couple of inches of rain the other day.

You know, when you don't have so much rain, you can forget how it works. You won't take an umbrella, you're stubborn, and then you do get wet and your shoes get soaked. You forget also how good the air smells when it's wet. You can go for a run without a jacket or hat, starting in a cold rain that warms up *with* your body, and you finish steaming. It is a day you'll have only once or twice a year.

I was walking last night in town with Will, our dog. I was trying to catch him not limping. He may have something wrong with his right front paw, or he may be fooling. Sometimes he holds it up and looks at you, sadly, but that's when you're leaving and he's staying home.

In almost every house we passed, in the dark, through the windows, we could see the Olympics on television. And there on a street corner four youngsters, wearing white shoes and sweatshirts, had set up their own race. Two of them, one a girl with a flashlight, waited on the sidewalk at a line they'd drawn. Twenty yards away, two boys got set and then dashed, yelling, to the finish, a laughing tumble on the grass. It's hard to know, really, if they were more inspired by the Olympics or by the commercials on the Olympics broadcast.

I think when you get older, you watch the Olympics in a different way. You watch a 1,500-meter race and see a runner win unexpectedly, and celebrate simply the pure exuberance of a youthful triumph. Or watch the same race and worry about Mary Decker Slaney losing badly after even more years of training and injuries and taking time to have a daughter. Later, she's talking about the games in Barcelona in 1992, and how she'll have to get started right away.

I've not always been happy with the coverage of the Olympic Games. I don't need to see *every* boxing match. I don't want to see just the Americans competing. I don't think the word "medal" should be a verb.

But last night we got to see pretty good coverage of kayak

racing on the Han River north of Seoul. Greg Barton of Homer, Michigan, in the thousand-meter race, came from behind to win a gold medal by ⅟₁₀₀th of a second. That was a long hard race, and ninety minutes later he was back paddling in the two-man kayak race. Again one thousand meters, and again by an inch, it seemed, he was in first place. Greg Barton, strong, happy, good-looking, two gold medals. I haven't seen any of the canoe racing yet, probably won't. I recall it from the Los Angeles games, the paddlers on one knee in long narrow canoes, a sort of competition seen mostly in Europe.

This week I drove south along the Saint Croix River and then the Mississippi, a good chance to go talk about canoe racing and fast boats in general. The Wenonah Canoe Company was started about twenty years ago in Winona, Minnesota; small town, small company. Today they sell three thousand canoes a year: fiberglass, Kevlar, composites.

There was a boat trailer outside the plant, waiting to be loaded. It would take fifty new canoes and kayaks to Seattle. Inside the shop it's all handwork, with wood and resin and green and gold strands of fiberglass. It looks like a design workshop at Lucasfilm, with models and prototypes sitting around.

Mike Cichanowski is the founder. I asked him about the Olympics. He sells a lot of boats that win a lot of races in this country—J-series canoes, kayaks—used by triathletes and marathon racers. But he has no boats in Korea for the summer games. That's a different kind of racing, with European boats and techniques, sprints rather than long distance. Mike has talked with the Olympic Canoe Committee, and there's a chance he could someday build the flat-water sprint boats designed for the games.

The way I figure it, Mike Cichanowski probably missed seeing Greg Barton win the kayak races on television. Mike was traveling yesterday to go canoe racing himself, in Hawaii. Forty-foot outrigger sea canoes, six people paddling. His two daughters, Amy and Heather, are also national champion canoeists.

All of this made me want to go right home and put my own boat in the water. There is something they try to explain about canoes, a concept called "motion pleasure." Mostly it means it's a whole lot more fun doing it than watching it. And this idea—doing as compared with watching—has been with me for a while this week. The space shuttle launch Thursday morning became part of it.

Then I heard a friend yesterday evening—a radio producer—talking by satellite phone from an advance base camp on Mount Everest, at seventeen thousand feet. I was worried about him, he sounded exhausted, breathless. It was good to hear his voice, but I wanted to be there with him. A while back, you might recall, we saw live television from the summit of Mount Everest, of a successful Japanese expedition. It did not seem right to be there by means of television. It was much too easy.

Once several years ago I was with a documentary news crew working on a radio story about a community down in east Kentucky. We were invited to church one Sunday morning, a service of the Old Regular Baptist Church. There was an objection from an elder who didn't want us to record the service. He said he had seen once, in a store in

Detroit, a record of an Old Regular Baptist service, which someone had made and was now trying to sell. And he said to me, "I didn't think it was right to be doing that. The Gospel happens here, at this time. It's not right to take it away."

I thought about it for a couple of hours and said, in my mind, amen.

I t's been chilly, and it's surprising to see the cold here in Tennessee, approaching frost, when the leaves on the trees are still mostly in full summer green. One leaf on a tree, one tree on a hillside, perhaps, may have turned. The leaves won't change colors for another ten days. We have come too soon. I've read that during October in the Great Smoky Mountains National Park, south and west of here some seventy miles, they're estimating that two million people will come through, mostly for the leaves.

My wife, Neenah, and I took a day this week and went for a pretty good hike in the Smokies. We left the car down on the main road leading over the mountains from Cherokee, North Carolina, to Gatlinburg, Tennessee. We put on boots and shorts, took parkas and lunch and water in a day pack, and started up the Alum Cave Bluffs Trail. We were thinking about possibly going all the way to the summit of Mount Leconte, 6,593 feet.

But that would be a ten-hour round trip, about, and we had a late start. I had gotten awfully interested in a sausage and eggs and biscuits and gravy and grits breakfast, with orange juice and coffee and a couple of newspapers. The meal was redemption for supper the night before, an experience that had proved conclusively—for me, anyway—that nothing good can happen to a rainbow trout inside a microwave oven.

We walked beside a creek, starting up the mountain. Much of the walking you'll do in the Smokies is *with* rushing water. The trees are mostly hemlock evergreens, some quite tall, lots of yellow birch, the bark peeling and golden in the sun. Close to the creek there are thickets of rosebay rhododendron.

This summer has been the 150th anniversary of the "Trail of Tears," the removal of the Cherokee Indians from their land on the southern edge of the Smokies. It was a march, forced by the government, to Oklahoma. Thousands of Cherokee died. They had been living in the foothills of the Smokies as mountaineers, as settlers with farms and markets and roads, with a written language and a government.

But gold was found nearby. The summer of the march, 1838, hundreds of Cherokee people went to hide up in the mountains, where it was reported that the underbrush was so thick the soldiers couldn't track them, not even with dogs.

Along the trail, about a mile and a half up, is Arch Rock. Then it's another two miles to Alum Cave. I miss our dog. Will loves to hike, to run up the trail and then look back, protecting us. But he's home, and this is bear country anyway. These fall days, they say, the bears can be seen in the treetops—find an oak tree, look up, see a couple of bears trying to eat a winter's supply of acorns. There are also wild boars in the park, and wild hogs, really a nuisance, some weighing up to three hundred pounds.

At Alum Cave the views begin to open up. We can see to the west and some to the north. The mountainsides and valleys spread out like a green rumpled blanket.

There are dead trees along the ridges, gray branches and snags. We saw them along the Blue Ridge Parkway too, down in North Carolina. It's acid rain damage, ozone pollution. The red spruce, especially, have been dying for ten years now. There's also an insect attacking the big Fraser fir trees that grow high up, the European balsam wood aphid. The trees have to be sprayed by hand.

I first saw the Smokies in the 1950s. Today they seem smaller, not as colorful and vivid, the forests less dense. We pass by and under the Alum Cave Bluffs—large sandy overhangs, water dripping from above. We go on up, looking for a place to have lunch, figuring we couldn't now make the summit and back down within daylight. I think I'm beginning to feel the altitude some.

We go on around a tricky part of the cliffs, holding on to cables. Along a ridge, and then a turn, and there's Mount Leconte high above. You can identify the outcropping known as Cliff Tops. That's where climbers go to watch the sun set, over several states.

This is the land that Horace Kephart called "Far Appalachia." Kephart was a librarian and historian. He came here at the turn of the century, in desperate need of adventure. He was looking for blank spaces on the map. He found the land and lived "back of the beyond" with the mountains and the people. Kephart was to write a valued book about the region, *Our Southern Highlanders.* And in 1921, in a preface to a revised edition, he wrote:

> Nine years have passed since this book first came from the press. My log cabin on the Little Fork of Sugar Fork has fallen in ruin. The great forest wherein it nestled is falling, too, before the loggers' steel. A railroad has pierced the wilderness. A graded highway crosses the county. There are mill towns where newcomers dwell. An aeroplane has passed over the county seat. Mountain boys are listening, through instruments of their own construction, to concerts played a thousand miles away.

Kephart's book is mostly anecdotal. He relates a lot of stories of the mountains, doesn't offer much about where these people came from, and that's something I always wonder about. A couple of my ancestors must have passed close by here, coming up from the Carolinas into Kentucky. When I was growing up, we had the idea that our people—the Appalachian forebears back in England, Scotland, Ireland—were of lower class and intelligence. There's been much research of late to dispel that notion.

There was a moment the other night that I still find curious, a connection, somehow, with the past. We were in a small town in the western North Carolina highlands. We stayed at an old inn where they offered a family-style dinner, lots of folks around a table with lots of food. Just as the applesauce and the creamed chicken and scalloped potatoes were almost gone, we heard piano music start up in the next room.

The music was loud and not hesitant, a performance of *Rhapsody in Blue.* Who could be playing the piano—that music—with so much confidence? Did this happen every night? Was it a tape? Or, maybe, a player piano?

We had dessert and coffee, said goodnight. All that took some time, and when we got into the parlor, the music was finished. And there was a Steinway grand player piano, the piano roll Gershwin's *Rhapsody in Blue,* part 1.

Something else that's intrigued me on this trip—those mileage indicators they have at restaurants and gift shops. The ones where you spin a wheel and read the mileage from here to Rock City, for example—174. To Atlanta—212. To Washington, D.C.—276.

If you could spin one of those wheels, and it would tell you the future, would you do it? If it could tell you how many years or days until the best meal of your life? How long until the birth of your youngest child? How much time until your happiest moment? Would you do it? What if the number would be a minus? What if it's already happened?

We're walking along the trail pretty fast and I'm out of breath now, in search of a lookout spot I'm trying to recall from the last time I was here, fifteen years ago. And there, by the trail, is the perfect place for lunch. It's still cold out but the sun is shining warmly on a grassy bank, and we settle back with crackers and cheese and peanut butter, pears, cool water, and not really any conversation.

We are at five thousand feet and pleased: altitude gained on foot is rewarding. The air is clear now, but soon the sun will start down over the ridge and the misty smoke of the mountains will rise.

I t's clear and frosty cold in the mornings, as low as eight degrees up north in Minnesota in the small town of Embarrass. But the days have been warm, with golden light and leaves, and kids coming home from school laughing and fussing at one another, and dogs barking just to hear themselves. I go out into the garden just after 7:00 A.M., wearing gloves and a hat and jacket. I take along a cup of coffee that steams in the sun.

This garden—just a bit of land, only four feet wide and

thirty feet long—has been my favorite place since the middle of May, when we had someone come by with a Rototiller and turn the soil over for the first time. Today I want to plant some daffodils and tulips out by the fence and around the forsythia bushes in front of the house. A couple over by the elm tree will be a surprise after the snow. And I'll plant some in the soft garden bed, plant them in appreciation and for good luck, even though I'll have to dig up the bulbs in late spring after they bloom.

I have a bulb planter, bought some years ago in a store that sold outdoor things and farm supplies. We lived in an apartment then in a city, and I was kidded a little about not ever even needing such a thing and who would have time anyway, but I used it that fall and the next, and have by this time planted daffodils in five front yards. Now this one's our own.

Last Sunday Neenah and I came back from traveling down to Tennessee. I watched a baseball game on TV, read the papers, sleepy on the couch. Early Monday morning we got to work putting the garden away for the winter. We had left town on the morning of the first hard freeze, and returned to downed tomatoes, fallen marigolds, most of them blackened and burned. Our "four o'clock" flowers must have gone down fast, they're flattened and limp. These are flowers from seeds from flowers from seeds from an island off the Adriatic coast of Yugoslavia. There, they tell me, the blossoms open at four o'clock in the afternoon. Ours opened on Central Daylight Time, in the mornings. We'll save the seeds from the plants, although there's now no way to tell which ones will grow fuchsia flowers and which will be yellow.

We had one splendid dark-red zinnia. It's dead. The pumpkin vine, a nonproductive show-off, has quit pretending. But the orange blossoms are still bright. Some garden mums, the purple ones, might make it. The Italian parsley looks fine, and the oregano and thyme and rose-scented geranium. We'll take them inside.

We start pulling up the marigolds and the tomato plants. The smells are overwhelming, pungent, sweet, acrid. One sadness of winter is that the smells are gone; you can't walk outside and brush your hand against the sage leaves, or cilantro.

The leeks are still okay, and the dill. The cherry tomatoes fall off the vines and lie there like jewels, red and green and yellow on the black uprooted dirt. The pansies have not been bothered by the frost. They seem so fragile, but they're thriving—some are deep maroon, some all white, a few heliotrope with white and yellow centers, some purple and black and yellow with blue centers.

The pansies grow in the best square foot of the garden, which is part of an old narrow driveway reclaimed for soil now rich and loamy, spiked with white-and-green-striped grass, one edge skirting the rough bark of an old elm tree stump. The flowers get some direct low evening light here, as the sun moves from south to west.

It's the same sunlight I used the other afternoon to warm up some yeast, dissolved in water and a bit of sugar. I was making bread, and put the mixing cup on the counter in a spot of sunlight, a sunbeam. I felt as though I were in a Walt Disney movie.

At this time in years past, the season's change into autumn, I have thought about those people in history who were isolated, and whose lives necessarily changed with the weather, who stayed cold until the spring and who would not have a fresh green vegetable for half the year. You can quite often now hear the sentiment that it is so much better for you to deal with things, foods especially, in season and in their own place. Asparagus only in the early spring and from nearby. Local peas in June, tomatoes in August, and apples into the late fall. I certainly agree with all this in principle. But the last person I heard going on about it was drinking a cup of coffee made with beans from Colombia.

There is a bird feeder in the garden. The black-capped chickadees delight in sunflower seeds from the feed store. We've put out some thistle seeds too, although that's more appreciated in snowy, colder weather.

What I really would like to see show up is an owl. There's an old wooden garage, big as a barn, out in back of the garden, that would make a fine home. It's dark and quiet inside; the owl would be safe and hunt for mice and talk to me in the evenings.

About twenty years ago I read a book, most of it in *Sports Illustrated* first, by William Service called *Owl.* A family in North Carolina finds a baby screech owl in the woods, takes it in, feeds it crickets and moths and hamburger disguised as a mouse. The owl also likes oranges and salad greens, and once at Sunday brunch it attacks—from above, with yellow eyes and feathers flared—a piece of tomato on the mother-in-law's plate.

The owl is happy in the house; it chitters and whirs and flies up the stairs and glides down them, and does a "dance of vexation around a brown snake in a glass jar." The family buys a trap that catches mice, unharmed, and William Service found a Schopenhauer quotation appropriate: "The pleasure in this world, it has been said, outweighs the pain. Or at any rate, there is an even balance between the two. If the reader wishes to see shortly whether this statement is true—let him compare the respective feelings of two animals, one of which is engaged in eating the other."

I like this idea from the book: in the morning you can put an owl in a kitchen cupboard, shut the door, and when you come back home and open the door, there the owl will be, looking at you. During the day you can take great satisfaction knowing that the owl is waiting for you, there in the dark.

And then this week I went to visit an owl—a barred owl that had been rescued and healed and now lives in a green shed with a shingled roof and wire sides. This owl has bars of colors down the breast, feathers with bands of brown and gray and white. It watches me with large brown eyes, with confidence. Its face is made up of concentric circles around eyes and beak, like unmoving ripples in a pool of water. The owl looks powerful but is mostly feathers. They say if you poke your finger in, you go a long way before you find a bird. The ears are hidden, efficient. They will hear a mouse under a foot of snow.

The barred owls and great gray owls, out by the Saint Croix River, will find evergreen trees and perch there, watching the weather change, listening for what is moving, waiting for winter's end.

The daffodils, mixed yellow from a bag of forty, and some white tulips, "late-blooming triumphators," go into the ground, like prayers. Planted with a wish: see you in the springtime.

22 October

27 degrees

The barometer reading 29.90 and steady

I n the darkness before sunrise comes the first early cold
fog of the year. It's been blustery, rained all night Wednesday and through the morning. With the wind last weekend,
then the rain, most of the leaves are gone. The radio says
there are snow showers up in the northeastern part of Minnesota.

Early one day this week, I went down to the feed store
in town. It's an old store a block or so away from the Saint

Croix River. You pull up and park out front, carefully, because it's a nice place—for ducks; easily a hundred of them. They come up in the morning from the water, politely looking for breakfast. They stand in the road outside the store: mallard ducks, the females brown, the males glossy green.

Inside, at the counter, I ask, "What is it they want?" And the guy says, "Cracked corn." I get some suet for the bird feeder, it's cold enough now for it. I buy some cat food and the biggest bag of dog food I can carry. It's forty pounds, and Will, our fifty-pound black, white, and tan "random breed," loves to see me coming in the house with it. We put the bag down in the basement. I carry, he supervises. I tear open the top. It's fresh, smelling of corn. He's got food for almost the whole winter, if it's supplemented with toast and peanut butter. Our cat, Sally, likes to be in the kitchen in the mornings when toast is being made, just to see the dog make a fool of himself.

If you leave the feed and grain store and walk north along the street by the river, you can see where a railroad line once ran. This town used to be a lot busier, down by the tracks, by the waterfront. I've walked before over to the trees at the edge of the river, and followed the path of the old train. That line came in from the south and would have curved here to the west, joining the tracks from the east.

The eastern line is still active. You can hear diesel freights coming past, most nights, in a slow, clanking rumble. It's a sound your mind will hardly notice, if you grew up along a river and in a railroad town.

The diesels were mostly new when I was little, in Ashland, Kentucky, and the tracks for the passenger line only three blocks away. The depot was about six blocks away, and it was my grandfather's favorite place to go. He'd get the out-of-town papers and talk to the stationmaster, maybe a conductor. My grandfather worked for a steel company, in the office. But he had wanted to be a railroad man and would have been a good one.

I have been more fond of trains in theory than in practice. You don't really get that much of a chance to ride them. The Amtrak to New York hardly counts. I always wanted to ride over the Rockies, or along the Pacific coast. I did travel overnight once on the Montrealer, up into Vermont, but I didn't sleep well. And once on the Southern Crescent, Washington, D.C., down to New Orleans. But it was too crowded to even get a sandwich or a cup of coffee. Still, though, it's the right speed at which to travel, the right rhythm.

There's a train I'd like to take sometime—the Cardinal—that runs out of Washington into Virginia, then south through the Shenandoah Valley to Clifton Forge, turning to cross the mountains of West Virginia. White Sulphur Springs, Charleston, Huntington, West Virginia; Catlettsburg, Ashland, Kentucky; Portsmouth, Ohio; then on to Cincinnati.

Here on the Saint Croix River, along the tracks, a light rain starts. It looks more like late November, but the air still smells sweet like green trees and nuts. You can smell oil too, and the water. The tracks run out to pass an old wooden freight depot, and then to cross the river. There's a steel bridge, painted black, low on the water. It swings aside to let the larger boats pass. That's about a mile away, and it's hard to get closer. "No Trespassing" signs are up everywhere; it's just a work yard now.

I walk up to the freight building. Some cars and trucks are parked outside. I shouldn't be here, but the face I see through the window is a friendly one, a man wearing a railroad cap. I go around the other side of the building and back out of the yard and into the town again.

One time my grandfather took my twin brother and me down to the train station, early on a Saturday. And with a friendly conductor's help, we climbed up into the train. They had a compartment where they would show cartoons, black and white sixteen-millimeter cartoons, and children traveling would watch them and stay quiet.

While the train was there in the station, we sat down to watch the Mickey Mouse cartoons, and my grandfather went off into the depot. When he came out, the train was gone, and we were gone with it. The next station was twenty miles up the line. He stood there, knowing he would have to call his wife and his daughter, our mother, and tell them he'd lost the twins.

I have a picture of my grandfather that I treasure, taken when he was younger than I am now, a handsome man, with almost a smile. But in my memory he is usually older, standing on the train platform with his cane, a brown suit and vest, a hat, and an unlit cigar in his hand; looking confused, looking east after the train taking away his grandsons; knowing he was going to be in big trouble at home; saying to himself, "I don't guess I should have done that."

I t's still plenty dark now, when I'm up in the mornings. The sun rose today at 7:47. It'll be good to have that moved back an hour, with daylight saving time changing. We had two strong nights and early mornings of moonlight Monday and Tuesday. The "hunter's moon" of October. On November 9th it will be the "new moon of the freezing" and then just before Thanksgiving it's the "beaver moon." The beavers by this date, the Indians noticed, had their houses ready and full of food.

The first snow was on Sunday. I went out about twelve o'clock; it had been raining and a neighbor was burning leaves. And you could see and smell the snow, through the warm smoke in the air.

The willow tree, out of my bedroom window, is still pale yellow and green. A ginkgo tree nearby is dropping golden leaves. The lilac bushes and small trees have most of their leaves yet. But they're darkening, turning almost purple, about to fall.

I checked with the University of Minnesota Arboretum. The last shrub in this part of the country to bloom every year is the witch hazel. Witch hazel would be neat to have in your backyard. An extract from the bark has some medicinal value, a witch hazel branch is often used for divining, "witching," a source of water. The flowers of the shrub, now in blossom, are yellow and resemble, they say, the straggly hair of a witch—a good flower for Halloween.

One of the Halloween creatures has been around in the evenings of late, our friend the bat, flying low through the trees at dusk. I only know of one poem about bats—it's by Theodore Roethke:

> *By day the bat is cousin to the mouse*
> *He likes the attic of an aging house*
>
> *His fingers make a hat about his head*
> *His pulse beat is so slow we think him dead*
>
> *He loops in crazy figures half the night*
> *Among the trees that face the corner light*

*But when he brushes up against a screen*
*We are afraid of what our eyes have seen*

*For something is amiss or out of place*
*When mice with wings can wear a human face*

We have a bird for Halloween too, I was thinking, looking out the window at the feeder full of sunflower seeds and at a contented male cardinal perched there. He looked like a trick-or-treater, with a sporty red cap and cape and a bandit's black mask.

My cardinals have been around about three weeks now. And it is my notion that perhaps we are seeing each day the same two birds. The male cardinal and the prettier, if not as showy, female cardinal, light brown with streaks of red. Often they will be together, one on either side of the feeder. We tend to think of them as a couple, and it's quite possible they are. Cardinals do stay together, and stay during the winter. There's probably a nest nearby in the bushes; she'll be laying eggs in the spring.

The cardinals are said to be the first to sing in the mornings, although I haven't heard them. They also, I've read, like to engage in "reflection fighting," a mock bird fight with their image in a mirror or a window. It doesn't really seem all that different from what we humans do sometimes, standing there in the morning in the bathroom arguing with ourselves in the mirror.

It's nice that the cardinals are setting up housekeeping, just outside. When the weather changes, you tend to think more about people, and birds and animals, being safely tucked away, settling down in warm places, sheltered from the cold and the dark.

We are only a few inches away from the weather and the world. A few boards, some bricks, a bit of plaster. We are a few centuries away from being sheltered only by trees and rocks. On Halloween, if you are whimsical enough, you could think of trick-or-treaters as creatures out there in the dark, goblins surely, and wolves and bears. And we stay huddled inside the shelter, throwing out scraps of food and candy to appease them.

There's a house close by that makes me wonder about our concepts and traditions of home. It's a house on Summit Avenue in Saint Paul, the most impressive of the Gilded Age houses there. I first saw it, I guess, about six years ago, and only this week made some time to go by for a visit. It's the James J. Hill House, finished in 1891, built by Mr. Hill and his wife, Mary, who was described once as "Mary Mehegan, a pretty little Irish waitress in the Merchant's Hotel downtown." Their new home stood on the edge of the bluff overlooking the Mississippi River.

A house of brick and steel beams and slate and marble and Massachusetts brownstone, a place to raise a large family. Four daughters were married here, made their entrances down the grand central staircase. The James J. Hill House is thirty-six thousand square feet. Its owners gave a party once for two thousand people.

Mr. Hill was the founder of the Great Northern Railroad, and was a strong and particular man. He wanted electric lights, even then, and wood-burning fireplaces—also gas fireplaces with ceramic logs. Maple floors, oriental carpeting, woven for this house in Turkey. All the woodwork hand carved from eastern white oak. He had his own mushroom cave, two walk-in safes, a theater on the fourth floor for the children, forced air heating from two immense coal-fired boilers in the basement. Mr. Hill owned a coal mine down in Iowa.

I thought the house would be awfully uncomfortable, but it's pleasant inside, with clean lines and thoughtful design. It's now a museum, so you can wander through and spend some time wondering, what would it have been like to live here? I went into the art gallery, Mr. Hill called it a "picture gallery," built for his collection, mostly paintings of nature by members of the Barbizon School. The room has a professional look. The ceiling is frosted skylights, and there is a suspended rectangular wooden frame to hold light bulbs. A curtain could be drawn, horizontally, across the skylight.

I try to imagine it . . . I would come in here after dinner. Someone would bring me a brandy on a silver tray. I'd light a cigar—a lot of my fantasies involve smoking a good cigar. I'd stand appreciatively for a long moment in front of Corot's *Springtime of Life.* Then I'd pat my English setter on the head and move to the end of the room to sit at the console of my pipe organ, built by George Hutchings of Boston—a tracker organ, 1,006 pipes. I'd nod to the butler, who'd signal Mike the fireman down below to start pumping the bellows, and I'd play the overture to *Carmen,* by Bizet. The dinner guests would gather in the doorway, smiling in admiration. And the doorbell would ring. . . . I wonder what James J. Hill and his wife gave out to trick-or-treaters on Halloween?

5 November

34 degrees

The barometer reading 29.54 and rising

The first sound I hear in the dark is the cat, Sally, outside. Most mornings these days I go downstairs and open the door and say, "I told you so." She walks in, covered with wet snow, with a disdainful glance at the dog, who has managed to spend most of the night on our bed. I put some water on for coffee, find an old towel. And Sally, who usually doesn't ever want to be picked up, lets me wrap her in the towel and purrs as I dry her ears and the thick fur around her head. I hold her against my chest, her stomach flat against mine.

Last night I had to dry off the dog, we'd been out for a run in a good splashy rain and came back to find the towel quick before . . . well, haven't you always wanted to do something, anything, as satisfying as it must be to a dog to come in the house and shake the rainwater off? He had been having me do tricks. We came in the yard the back way, and there's a gate there, one of those folding gates about fifteen inches high, to keep him from getting out. From the kitchen window I've seen Will jump that gate easily, going after a squirrel, but he doesn't know that I know he can do it, and so he insists, always, that I bend over and pull the gate back so he can walk into his backyard.

The other morning we were in the car going to work. We got a couple of blocks away and thought maybe we'd left the iron on. Turned around, went back in the house, and found the dog already upstairs, sleeping with the cat on the extra bed. There's not much you can say. You just shake your head and go on with whatever sort of life your pets are going to allow you to have.

With everybody fed and dry and happy, I sit in the kitchen and watch the snow, wet and heavy, blowing from the north. A storm system is passing slowly there. My calendar says November 2nd was the official beginning of the freezing rain season. It's been dark in the early evening. The leaves are gone from the trees now. And it's quieter, many of the birds have left, and a lot of animals and insects have gone into hibernation.

The black bears up by the Canadian border went to sleep long ago. The snakes have found hiding places, the spiders are safe, wrapped in their own silk. The box elder bugs are tucked away in the bark of trees. And the leopard frogs have gone to the bottom of the lakes, before the ice comes. There are lots of woodchucks asleep in this part of the country. They would win a blue ribbon for hibernation, comfortable underground, breathing once in five minutes, their heart rate down to four beats a minute. It is said they sleep so deeply you could take one, curled up in a ball, and roll it across the floor without its waking up.

Poison won't work on hibernating animals. And I've read that a scientist once amputated the leg of a sleeping squirrel; the squirrel didn't awaken, and bled only a few drops. The long sleep of hibernation is a death in a way. For survival, a defense against winter.

On Thursday it was clear and warm, and I spent most of the day in the car, driving north, listening to seventies rock on the radio and warnings about the weather: "It'll be rain for Friday night football, and snow for the deer hunt Saturday." This morning was the opening of Minnesota's deer season. I wanted to visit a lighthouse up on Lake Superior's shore, to make the trip before November's weather comes. The Split Rock lighthouse, an hour north from Duluth, is built on a promontory. The waters of the lake are eight hundred feet deep, just out from the cliff. And beneath the water there, the ship *Madeira* lies—she went down in 1905.

The storms of November are known on Superior by the names of ships. November 10th, 1975, is called the Fitzgerald storm. The Matafa storm was the one in 1905, thirty ships were lost, and the *Matafa* went under just outside the harbor in Duluth. The Split Rock lighthouse was built soon after as a bearing light.

I arrived just before five o'clock, and right at sunset I followed a path down to a rocky beach. It probably always has been a landing site. In earlier years Ojibway canoes would have been here, then later the cargo canoes of the voyageurs. And in 1910 the lighthouse supply boats started stopping by. Along about the end of November every year the boats would come to take the lightkeepers and their families to town for the winter. The lighthouse, pale yellow and dark green, is above, at the edge of the cliff. It's been restored.

This could be an evening in 1924. It's quiet, the wind is down, the birch trees are shining. Lake Superior is so vast it could be an ocean. I wonder about the lake and what it's like beneath the waters. Spirits, and dreams, and songs; the water noisy and rolling during a storm; and the light: a fearful yellow, and it's forever cold.

I walk up the hill, and there's a house with people in the kitchen and a couple of dogs come out to say hello, Ozzie and Polly, golden retrievers, the lightkeeper's dogs. He isn't really a keeper. The light was shut down, decommissioned years ago, and Lee Radzak is officially the site superintendent. Split Rock is a state park now. But Lee would have been a good lightkeeper. He likes the machinery, the responsibility; he respects the water. He's been here seven years with his family, probably enjoys the winters best, in the cold and quiet.

We walk over in the dark to the side of the cliff, to the

foghorn station. Foghorns are mounted outside on the roof, driven originally by gasoline engines, then diesel. The horns are diaphonic, two tones, they could be heard seven or so miles away. But you couldn't depend on it—the sound waves would skip on the water, and you could be inside a silent zone and in quite a lot of danger. A pamphlet published in 1906 warned the Lake Superior captains: "Do not think you are out of hearing distance because you fail to hear a fog signal, nor that you are at a great distance because the sound is faint, nor that you are near because you hear the signal plainly."

We go over to the base of the lighthouse tower, unlock the door, and go into the watch room. Curved walls of white enameled brick; there's a small stove, a desk. Then we take the circular stairway up to the light itself.

The lantern assembly weighs six and a half tons, made in Paris; two lenses, designed by Augustin Fresnel. They are prisms that both reflect and refract. Even the light from a kerosene flame, as in the old days, could be seen at great distance. The whole assembly turns. It's mounted—floating—on liquid mercury.

We wind a crank, pulling some weights up through the center of the tower. It's like the mechanism of a grandfather clock. As the weights start winding down, slowly the lens begins to turn. Lee switches on the light itself—just a thousand-watt bulb—and the Split Rock lighthouse is again in operation, the lens rotating every twenty seconds. The lens is two-sided, so the light is seen by a ship—a flash—every ten seconds. The lighthouse keepers stood four-hour watches, listening to the clockwork machinery and the hiss of the

kerosene lamp, watching the lights flare out into the night.
The official distance the light carries is twenty-two miles. It
has been seen sixty miles away.

We lock up and go down the stairs. The light will stay
on, turning for a couple of hours until the weights wind
down. I start thinking out loud about the darkness, and the
isolation here, thinking about the movie *The Fog.* Lee has
seen it, oh sure, and *The Shining,* he says, did you see that?
But those are only movies. The light is real, and the lake.
And the storms that will come soon, the ice and wind, the
memories of fatal shipwrecks.

We stand down on the cliff and watch the beams of white
light easily flowing out through the dark and an early evening fog. The light flashes in reassurance. Lee tells me the
coast guard asked him to adjust his light, to take its beam just
off the horizon and make sure he only lights it at unpredict-
able intervals. On the navigation charts for Lake Superior,
Split Rock is identified as an "abandoned lighthouse."

Next Thursday, at sunset on the tenth of November, Lee
Radzak will climb the tower, wind the gears, and turn on
the light, in tribute to the men of the *Edmund Fitzgerald,*
who passed here out of Duluth for the last time thirteen
years ago, sailing into a storm.

It's snowing outside and quiet. It's become a world you could paint with two colors: the trees, the fences, black and shades of gray, the snow, wet and soft and white.

We've all been talking about snow. It's apparently a favorite topic in this part of the country every Veteran's Day. There was a pretty good snowstorm here in 1940. November 11th was Armistice Day then. It was a Monday. The day started warm and got cold fast, and windy and snowy. Sixteen inches in Minneapolis. Twenty-six at Collegeville, not far west. Fifty-nine people were said to have died in Minnesota through that day and night, the next morning. The temperature went down to almost zero.

There's a book of recollections of the storm, put together by William H. Hull: *All Hell Broke Loose: Experiences of Young People During the Armistice Day 1940 Blizzard.* Some of the stories are quite sad, but most have happy endings. And all of them have interesting titles. For example:

— Roasted Mallard Satisfied Our Hunger
— I Made an Eighteen-Hour House Call
— Burn Anything to Keep the Baby Alive
— We Spent Three Nights in the Packard
— His Clothing Just Stood There on Its Own
— Bourbon for Half-Frozen Accountant
— Boy Friend Slept in Baby's Crib
— So Busy My Pockets Were Stuffed with Money
— Your Feet Are Still Cold, Says Husband
— The Girl and the Snowbound Marine
— Men Shovelled Three Miles for Cigarettes

A few weeks ago, just before Halloween, I was talking about bats—bats looking like trick-or-treat creatures. I read a poem about bats. And since then I've been getting bat poetry in the mail, including these lines by D. H. Lawrence:

*Wings like bits of umbrella*
*Bats*

> *Hanging upside down like rows of disgusting old*
>   *rags*
> *And grinning in their sleep*
> *Bats*
> *In China the bat is symbol of happiness*
> *Not for me!*

I bring this up again because now we have a bat in the basement. I turned on the light at the top of the basement stairs the other evening—I never go down in a basement without pausing to look first—and I thought I saw a rat running across the floor, fast and black. But it seemed too fast. Then I heard a squeaking noise and a fluttering, and the *bat* flew, more slowly, back across the basement. I shut the door and went into the kitchen to make the announcement.

We stood there for a while, engaging in all sorts of conjecture about the bat and what a desperate, violent end our lives would come to should we ever try to go down into the basement again. Probably the cat was already dead down there, the blood draining from her neck. We thought of a cross, against the evil. A friend stopped by, suggested a tennis racket. I thought at least I could wear a rain parka with a hood and gloves, maybe coax the bat outside.

Bats are the only mammals that fly. Some bats do drink blood or nectar, but not the one in our basement, which is most surely the variety called the "little brown bat." It eats insects. Bats maneuver and find their prey by *echolocation,* using mostly noises so high that we can't hear them. Some people like bats enough to put up a house for them in the backyard, but these animals have sharp teeth and could have rabies. So don't handle bats or keep them for pets, the books say.

I think I knew that much already. The bat is probably looking for a cold place, between thirty and forty degrees, to spend the winter. It will hang upside down and wait until a day in springtime when I go down in the basement to do some laundry and I've completely forgotten about it. That's when they like to get you.

Yesterday, with the weather changing, I wanted to walk out into the woods to see what green is left before the snow, and to take a good look at the trees now that all the leaves are down. I took the dog and we went along a trout stream that I know about. The wind was up and crackling through the branches. The birch and cottonwood trees were gray and clean against the sky. The temperature of the air was about forty. I touched my hand to the water. The cold stayed for a minute or two. But the mosses along the trail were still bright, and much of the grass. There were clumps of dark green stalks that I hadn't noticed before, in the summer. *Sedum equus*—called "horse's tail."

If you were a young boy and in the woods by the river, hiding from someone, you could use one of these stalks to breathe with underwater, if you had seen the right movies. And you would have a pocketknife, a good one but hard to open, some string, maybe a compass. You'd be wearing blue jeans, tennis shoes, a flannel shirt, a jacket. You've lost your gloves, but it's just you and your dog out for a walk before supper. You could hear your mother whistling for you a long way off.

There's a description I remember of being in the woods

as a very young boy. A first forest adventure alone. The author writes as a man, from memory:

> Soon I found myself in a dense part of the forest where the trees were taller and the path became lost. . . . I was completely isolated in the luxuriant, tangled growth of ferns which were well above my head. In my infant mind I seemed to have entered the fairyland of my dreams. . . . I could see shafts of light where the sunshine lit up the morning mists. . . . I began to walk faster, buoyed up with an almost ethereal feeling of well-being. . . . I sank to the ground in a state of ecstasy. . . . As I lay back a dead twig snapped, like the crack of a whip; the birds warbling sounded like the notes of a cathedral organ.

This is a memory from before the turn of the century in the countryside of England. The writer's name was Richard St. Barbe Baker. He was born in a house on the edge of the pine woods in the south of Hampshire. He became a forester, a conservationist. And he lived a very long life of commitment to trees—in Britain, Canada, Kenya, Palestine, the Soviet Union, this country. He made twenty trips to see the redwoods in California, and talked John D. Rockefeller into donating half a million dollars to save them.

It is said that St. Barbe Baker was responsible for the planting of twenty-six trillion trees. I had the honor of meeting him a few years ago. He talked with me about

Britain, about Africa, and about a dinner he had had with
Franklin Roosevelt. And he wished for me "the heart of a
pine, the strength of an oak, the endurance of the redwood
tree."

St. Barbe Baker was ninety-three years old then. He was
aware of his diminishing life. He was being taken care of by
three young people, almost strangers, who loved him. He
had come from New Zealand for a ceremony at the Redwoods National Park, had listened to the speeches and the
music, and had sat in his wheelchair afterward talking with
children about the trees. He had white hair and wore a green
cape, and seemed at times to resemble a tree. He often talked
with trees, sang to them.

As St. Barbe Baker got older, life became very simple, and
I think of it often, the way he lived. A daily, vital concern
for something important: shelter, food, a little warmth, some
music, a memory, a smile.

19 November

35 degrees

The barometer reading 29.93 and rising

A cold rain is falling, close to sunrise. The folks on the television said snow for another Saturday morning, two or three inches, but it's only rain.

Wednesday night we had dark clouds filling the Saint Croix River Valley as the sun went down, and rain and then snow, wind-driven, spitting. You could hear thunder to the south, then lightning, the low clouds over the river glowing white and yellow for an instant. The rain is heavier with continuous thunder today. It is all the weather you could want.

There is perhaps one morning during an entire winter when you manage to get the temperature in the bedroom just perfectly right. You've left the window open, there's a comforter on the bed, and in the shadowy light before sunrise, you understand that you're wonderfully warm inside the covers and breathing clean and cold air, and you've maybe got a good thirty minutes more to stay in bed, and even then you still won't have to hurry. Already you can hear crunching noises out on the road, and the wheels spinning in snow, but it will be clear and mostly melted by the time you have to go.

You have a perfect cup of coffee, some fresh orange juice and toast, read about pleasant things in the newspaper, laugh along with the radio, take a good hot shower, and notice in the mirror that you're looking a lot more rested these days. You find your best pair of jeans, warm from the dryer, and they're not as tight as they were only last week. Well, it's like I said. There's only maybe one morning a winter it happens that way.

In the town on these nights, with the rain and mist and snow in the air, you notice the lights more. Streams of frosted light shining up into the dark from the courthouse and the fire station. The white steeple of a church lit from within, with blue. Some of the big houses have Christmas lights already, garlands of green and red. And last night, when we opened the doors into the high school gymnasium, there was a *reverberance* of light and music and youth.

We had hurried through supper to get up to the school and the basketball game on time. It costs a couple of dollars to get in. They're selling popcorn, but that can wait, and anyway the sign says no food or pop in the gym. I'm looking for a home side and a visitors' side, but the band is over there, across the court, and it looks like the students are there too. The local parents, we discover, are sitting with the visitors, on our side.

They play the national anthem. There's a large American flag on the wall. The baskets look lower to me, for some reason, and I haven't noticed this before—there's padding along the bottom edges of the glass backboards. The scoreboard—red lights on gray and black—is set for eight-minute quarters. The referees are ready, striped shirts, black pants, black shoes. Referees can sometimes look so officious, the way they hold themselves, as if they're wearing corsets. The horn sounds, a bit too loud.

Ten young women come out, five in white, five in blue. Then the tip-off, and I guess for a moment—even though I watched the U.S. women's team, on television, win in Seoul at the Olympics—I was afraid this high school girls' game would be played by those ancient nonsensical rules. Remember? Two guards would bring the ball up the floor and then stand there and wait. Only the forwards could shoot.

The team in white is visiting. The blue team went to the state finals last year, but lost a superstar player. Both coaches, men, are wearing coats and ties. The players are wearing white and blue basketball shoes, Nike. The cheerleaders are wearing white and blue cheerleading shoes, the same brand. The play is fast, there are lots of mistakes. Number 15 blue takes a three-point shot and misses everything. The next time up the court, she tries again from the same place and hits it. The first period ends 9 to 7, blue.

The girls come to the bench. There are towels and squeeze bottles of water. The coach has a clipboard to diagram plays. His team watches, nodding. They are just young girls, and there is a look they get on their faces that they will use nowhere else in life.

The second quarter: Loomis, Evans, Dieckman, Kees, Fraylich, against Dierks, Peterson, Huftel, Kinney, Lundquist. Lots of scrambling and jump balls, lots of good-looking shots missing, and some awful shots swishing. It seems a lay-up is more difficult than a three-point shot. The home team in blue pulls ahead, and then way ahead. The cheerleaders, in blue, start talking to one another and looking around up in the stands. The band members start moving toward their places at the end of the grandstand.

Not far from here on Front Street, down by the river, there's a large old wooden barn, painted green, with a corrugated tin roof. It's now a lumber yard. Back in the spring I wanted some one-by-twos for the tomatoes and got to talking with one of the clerks, an older man. We went in back to pick up the wood, and he said, "Guess what this building used to be—see those numbers up there?" The numbers on the wall were for rows of seats, and in 1910 this was a boxing arena. Prizefighting, bare-knuckle fighting. And just for a couple of years there were big crowds, coming out on the weekends from the cities on special trains. The clerk remembers sitting high up there in the back as a young boy, watching the fights through the dust and yellow glare of the lights.

It's halftime. The band is playing "The Stripper," with lots of volume. We go outside, for popcorn and R-C Cola and peanut butter cups, and stand around looking at the trophy case and at the young people in blue jean jackets and blond hair with mousse. They all look so young. But then so do all the parents sitting in our section, they would have to have been married in junior high school.

The second half goes by quickly. The home team is in front 55 to 24 at the third quarter. The team in white does not let up, though, and playing against the blue team's second string makes a game of it for a while. Number 34, a guard, has four straight baskets, one of them a three-pointer. Then it's over, 63 to 42. The teams line up to slap hands in congratulation. Number 34 comes over to the stands, smiling, talking with four boys in letter jackets. They look like football players who will be farmers. The student managers gather up the balls and water bottles. Most people leave quickly.

I once tried being a play-by-play announcer for a radio station during one basketball season. I wasn't much good—I was always about two baskets behind—but it was lots of fun. And I remember well this moment: you learn to write down the final score of the game immediately; do it before you read the last commercial and do the wrap-up and interview the coach. You write it down because if you don't, you will say on the radio, "So good night from the Ashland High School gym, where once again the final score was . . ." And you look up, and they've turned off the scoreboard and left it blank.

You do that only once in your career. But you get through it and go on out into the fresh cold air, and go home along with everyone else in your town. Win or lose, it's Friday night.

D ownstairs in the kitchen, in the dark, I light the stove for coffee and open the back door. There's a warm wind, and in the sky to the southeast, the slightest crescent of a moon.

On Wednesday we had the first sullen day of winter. Dark skies, bitter, windy, and the streets were dirty, and the cars. I couldn't find anyone in a better mood than I was. You didn't want to watch the news, it was just bad fights and accidents. And at night, when I was out for a run, the dogs came out of the backyards, fast and silent. They didn't bite, but it would have been a good chance.

It's on days like this that I start to feel old, stiff. I find myself sitting, staring, sort of hunched over, like some old guy with long underwear and suspenders who would go three or four days without shaving, drinking instant coffee made with tap water, the newspapers outside the front door, no point in answering the phone.

But Thursday it was sunny again with frost sparkling, and the birds were back early at the feeder. I've named the male bird after the Nicaraguan poet Ernesto Cardenal, the female we call Maria. And I got to watch, out in the snow, little boys and girls in snowsuits and hats and mittens, with their moms and dads. They were helping shovel snow, with tiny red plastic shovels, and laughing.

We were away at Thanksgiving, visiting in the East, spending some time in the country. A night with a full moon, lighting the valley. A conversation with a hoot owl, far back in the woods.

The next morning, out for a walk, we followed a road up through a hollow, a place we hadn't been before, just on the eastern edge of the Blue Ridge Mountains. Several log cabin homes dotted the road. It was a pretty good climb. We stopped to rest on a stump by the road close by a small white house, kind of handmade looking. There was a woodpile, smoke coming from a stove pipe, a garden, a pickup truck.

The door of the house opens and three dogs run out, barking, yipping. One is all brown, mostly a corgi. Two are black and white, one a Chihuahua background, the other a Pomeranian mix. They want to see who can be petted the most.

Their owner comes out. He's a large, friendly man, surely in his eighties. He's wearing overalls, an old blue quilted jacket. A red cap. He shakes his head about the dogs. "Just can't control 'em," he says. He's had one of the dogs for a long time, the two others he found down at the county shelter. They are the best watchdogs, he says, "they'll run right at anything, even a bear." Bear season, I've read, starts Monday, a half hour before sunrise.

We comment on the nice bright morning and his garden, and he offers us some sallet greens. He's got plenty, just sowed it for a cover crop. He calls to the dogs, "Get on in," and they jump into the front of the pickup and then up to the top of the seat, and they all drive off down the road together—three dogs riding just behind the man's head— going to the store. "They like to ride," he said.

I was thinking about another older man this week, a man I met ten years ago. We were in his backyard to see his weather station, a wooden box on a pole. He kept a daily record and mailed it in to the weather service. Said it was something old men liked to do.

I remembered that conversation when I went out to spend some time at the National Weather Service, here at the airport. I was there in time for the one o'clock briefing. Fifteen weathermen, one woman, gathered in a room around computer screens, with maps spread everywhere.

The forecaster on duty explains the morning to those coming on shift, with talk of millibars and compressional

warming and long wave troughs, and atmosphere maps
showing the jet stream in purple at 130 knots. He's smiling
a bit, he had forecast some snow for a part of Minnesota, but
it didn't happen. But he's confident about warmer days
ahead, and then the chance of another Saturday with snow,
the weather moving in a seven-day cycle.

Afterward I ask him, when no one's looking or listening,
why the jet stream, and the weather, always moves from
west to east. The rainstorms, when I was growing up, always came over Mr. Buckley's house. The answer is simple.
There is cold Arctic air in the north. Warm southern air
moving that way is diverted by the rotation of the earth. In
the Southern Hemisphere the weather people are always
looking in the other direction. The winds aloft move from
east to west, south of the equator.

In just a little while some grade school children come
through on a tour, to learn this secret about the jet stream
at an earlier age. The forecasters call this a "Howdy Doody
Show" when the kids come by, and they explain their instruments and charts with patience and enthusiasm. My favorite
is the ceilometer. To measure the height of the cloud ceiling
at the airport, it bounces a laser beam up to the bottom of
the clouds and back down.

The most important forecasting tools are the weather
balloons, with instrument packages and transmitters on
board. They're released every day at 6:00 A.M. and 6:00 P.M.
from two places in Minnesota. Fifty or sixty balloons are
sent up each day from the United States, and hundreds more
worldwide, to rise above one hundred thousand feet and
send back the temperatures, wind speeds, air pressure. They

are how we know what weather is moving where and how fast. The instrument packages parachute back to earth; many of them are returned to the weather service.

Everyone seems to like the weather business, even though they work in shifts and say they never get used to the hours. It can be an exciting place, especially in the summer with thunderstorms and sirens going off. You can watch one screen and see every lightning flash across the state of Minnesota. Most of these people retain a fascination with weather that began, they say, with instruments out in the backyard.

Like my friend in Massachusetts. He lived on Martha's Vineyard, in Edgartown, was the editor of a weekly newspaper there, and in every issue he wrote about the weather and what had been happening early in the morning. Henry Beetle Hough was his name. His best-known book, *Country Editor,* starts this way: "On the morning the war began Betty and I were hurrying to get to the *Gazette* office as close to half past seven as possible. It was publication day. The northeaster appeared to have blown itself out, the sun was coming through the clouds in the east, and the air began to be sweet and clear as it so often is in the fall." Betty was his wife, and they lived in a white frame house with a succession of collies. The one I met was named Graham.

Betty had died a few years before my visit. Mr. Hough and Graham were alone together, getting up very early for a walk every morning at sunrise. He said he often felt Betty's presence in the house at night. Mr. Hough had sentences like these in his memory: "The air had lost the last of its winter harshness, and wrapped the morning in gentle peace—it carried the scent of the lilacs as if this were a special fragrance of the day."

You know, I think the thing of it is, you have to decide pretty much now what sort of old man you're going to be. And then hope to be lucky enough to get there.

I usually go out into the backyard with the dog, to check the other thermometer on the side of the garage. But I stay in this morning and sit in the dark kitchen listening to the radio. "Romance for String Orchestra, Opus 11," by Finzi, I'm told. And there's weather news. It's one degree also over in the Twin Cities. Tonight, up in the north of Minnesota, maybe thirty below.

It's my friend Mindy on the radio, from Saint Paul, sounding friendly, awake. But radio can still sound mystical to me, when it's just one person listening to one voice coming in from somewhere.

Will is sitting patiently on the kitchen floor, which is a bit chilly. I've given him an extra handful of food. What he wants, though, is to go back upstairs to the bedroom. There's someone still in bed who needs protection and warmth. But I've shut the door.

I heard on television the other night—part of a documentary about the mind—the theory that we as humans are the only species that makes plans. We are alone in considering the consequence of action. I'm not sure about that. The dog, it's clear, is planning to get back in bed, because he knows he will enjoy it.

I have been a bit concerned about one aspect of that theory, though: our ability to make plans and then worry about far too many things. I realize I've been trying to figure out how to send Christmas presents by Federal Express. And I'm sure that many people around the neighborhood are already thinking beyond the holidays. "Now just what day is it the city comes by to pick up the Christmas trees out by the street?"

It reminds me of a play I saw once. A mother and daughter fuss at each other. The mother is overly neat. The daughter complains, saying, "Well, mother, why don't you just have the paper boy throw the newspaper directly into the trash can?"

The other morning it was not quite so cold. It was sunny, the wind light. I had some time, I was encouraged by perhaps too much coffee. I'd been listening to some rock and roll—Wilson Pickett, from the sixties, "In the Midnight

Hour" and "Six, Three, Four, Five, Seven, Eight, Nine"—
and I decided to put the canoe on the car and see if I could
find some open water on the Saint Croix. I'd drive north to
where the river is still narrow, the current faster, keeping the
ice away.

The car is white, the canoe sort of a dirty yellow. I have
a red vest, polyester, a down coat, blue, a gray cap, a bright
orange life jacket. I am not a deer.

I'm wearing long underwear, two pairs of socks, hiking
boots. I'll take rubber knee-high boots for the river, and a bag
of dry clothes.

Fifty minutes later I drive down to the landing. We've
put our boat in here many times this year. Now, no one's
around. It's seventeen degrees, and well into December in
the North.

There's open water, but it's out there twenty feet away,
with ice in between. Ice leads away from the shore, white
and gray with bubbles and cracks. I can't try to walk out
there, can I, with the canoe? No, it would tip over, or the
ice would break. But a hundred yards away, the open water
comes up to the bank, it looks like.

Just have to get these boots on, get the canoe off the car,
put on the life jacket, pick up the paddle, pick up the canoe.
It's light at first, a solo canoe, sixteen feet six inches. To get
to the water over there, I have to cross some ice, an inlet of
the river, sort of like a lake. It looks safe, it looks thick.

On ice like this you can hear dark underwater sounds, and
cracking. They say you need twelve inches of ice to drive on,
five inches for snowmobiles, four for skating. How much do
you need for someone just walking with a light canoe, being

very careful, moving slowly? Or should I go fast in case it starts to break?

I make it to the other side and then struggle along the bank in deep snow, dragging one end of the canoe on the ice. I'm working pretty hard, and I can see the water's moving fast and my pulse rate is up and the ice can be sharp and I have too many clothes on. I can see the small item in the newspaper, way in the back, "Man Found on Icy River-bank." Although in the papers here they like to tell everyone how old you were when you were doing such a foolish thing. So it would be "Man, 46, Found on Icy Riverbank."

At last, the canoe is floating in the water. All I have to do is get in. The river bank is too high to do this right, but I hang on to a tree limb, trying to step straight down into the center of the boat. And I make the step and somehow get the other foot in, and the boat stops rocking.

It starts to drift. And the noise stops—the clattering and scraping and panting; it's quiet. And the boat moves, with the sunlight and the cold air, on the water. This is why I came.

Thin sparkling sheets of ice float on the surface. The current is strong. The canoe almost sweeps around the bends of the river. I realize I shouldn't go too far, though, and soon I put the paddle in the water for a hard turn, the bow coming around. Then it's an upstream fight for about thirty minutes. Zip open the life jacket, the coat, take off the gloves, start thinking about lunch.

I come back over to the bank and my tree limb and try to pull myself out, and slip. One foot goes in the water—it's deeper than I thought—then the other leg goes in. The water's up to my waist, filling my boots. I try to keep the canoe from floating away and find the paddle, and I'm real happy I got to be on the river some before this happened. And, finally, I pull myself up on the bank.

This is a fairly intense pain, this sharp, stabbing cold. It's interesting. I have to walk to the car, and maybe I'd better not take my boots off because in just a few minutes my feet will be numb anyway. The canoe's on the bank, safe. I drop the paddle, start back out over the ice toward the car, walking lightly. I almost feel like whistling.

Now I understand why I was thinking about the words from the Robert Service poem "The Cremation of Sam Magee." You remember, "Strange things done in the midnight sun / the Arctic trails, secret tales"? Sam Magee from Tennessee is looking for gold, but he can never get warm. On Christmas Day on the Dawson Trail he's dying and wants to be sure that his body will be cremated, he's "afraid of the icy grave." His buddy takes the corpse along on the sled to Lake Labarge, where he finds an old ship and builds a fire in the boiler. And he says, after a while:

> *And there sat Sam, looking cool and calm, in the*
> *heart of the furnace roar;*
> *And he wore a smile you could see a mile, and he*
> *said: "Please close that door.*
> *It's fine in here, but I greatly fear you'll let in the*
> *cold and storm—*
> *Since I left Plumtree, down in Tennessee, it's the*
> *first time I've been warm."*

Well, there's no danger here, really, on the banks of the Saint Croix. Not unless I break something or hit my head. The sun is shining and I've got extra clothes in the car. And I do have the car keys.

I'm shivering a bit now, and my legs are shaking. I get dried off and changed, go bring the canoe back, load up, and drive home, listening to the Wilson Pickett tape "Mustang Sally" and making plans for a hot bath.

There's no wind, and before dawn, the sky and the snow are both a pale blue.

We had about an inch of snow yesterday, without much notice. It just snows and the trucks come out, and people go on down the road. Monday evening we were coming back from Chicago, moving north and west in snow that was heading east. It was dark, and we were listening to country music on the radio, and I was driving probably too fast, but you get into a rhythm with it. The wipers were going and the snow was coming in low and direct to the lights, and you make sure you have your shoulder harness on and the heater turned down, just a little chilly, so you can stay awake.

Then I saw a truck in the ditch, jackknifed, and over the next fifty miles about ten cars in there too. And only half of the songs on the radio were any good, it seemed. If they're going to play an old Merle Haggard song, why wouldn't they play one of the good ones? And it's awful what you can get away with these days if you call it a Christmas song.

So I slowed down and drove my age, found the football game on the radio, and made plans for ordering a pizza once we got home safe and said hello to the dog.

Yesterday morning I drove by myself, south, along the Saint Croix River to the Carpenter Nature Center, just to spend some time out in the snow, on some trails where I hadn't been since summer. I parked and went inside the office, where the staff naturalists were sitting in front of computers. I rescued one, to take a walk with me. She put on boots and wool pants and a parka, and we went out into the orchard.

I asked if they'd been seeing eagles out over the river. She said the other day, down by the water, there were some eagles *fishing*. Most of the river is frozen over, but in some open water the eagles were splashing down for fish, and trying to catch the ducks that were swimming along. The eagles would dive; the ducks would duck, under the water, then come up looking around.

Here at the center they've been watching a red fox hunting. The fox walks carefully, listening, then hops up and bites down through the snow, catching field mice and meadow voles.

It's snowing quite a lot now, as we walk along the trail. The snow is wet and heavy. It could be wilderness out there, in the valley. The clouds could be mountains. It's just a bit too cold.

In the winter, in the woods, I always remember a book I read quite a few years ago called *Mountain Man.* Vardis Fisher wrote it, about a fellow before the turn of the century who spent his life hunting and trapping, wandering in the Rocky Mountains of Montana, Wyoming, and Idaho. He cared only about having a good knife, a horse, a few friends, and freedom. He would ride along, hungry in a bad winter up in the mountains in the snow, and he would think about food and about music. Recalling, for example, a breakfast of wild geese eggs, about a dozen, and elk steaks dripping in their hot juices, browned biscuits sopping wet with marrow fat from a bear, golden honey and huckleberry jam, a gallon pot of coffee. And to complete the reverie, he would play music in his mind, Beethoven piano sonatas in C major and F minor. Here on the ridge at the nature center, we are only minutes away from hot coffee and a bag of apple spice doughnuts that I brought.

Laurie tells me of a butterfly that spends the winter tucked away behind the bark of a tree. It's called the "mourning cloak" butterfly. It's soft brown, the wings have a midnight-blue edge. On warm days in the winter, it will come out and fly silently through the trees.

In the meadow there are grasshopper eggs, waiting for

spring; thousands of worker bees deep in the hive, around the queen; cedar waxwings, come to feed at the crabapple trees, the fruit rusty red and fermented. The birch trees are sending out their seeds, you can see the tiny winged seeds on the snow. Laurie reminds me, as we pass some aspens, that the buds are already out on all the trees, the buds for next spring's leaves. And the aspen buds indeed are there, so small and fuzzy I would never have noticed.

We follow the trail down to the river, past an old railroad line. The ice here seems finished—sturdy, with windblown snow. Beavers have felled silver maples and willows, some four or five inches around, gnawed them neatly in two, about a foot from the ground. The beavers are piling up construction material and getting lots to eat. They like the soft wood just under the bark.

Laurie says sometimes, when a beaver's nearby, you can smell anise in the air. We find a lodge by the edge of the water. I would have thought it was just a pile of sticks and logs, drifted up, but she points out the neatly chewed ends. This beaver is probably more than two years old, weighs over forty pounds, gets into the lodge by swimming under the ice, and most likely would not appreciate visitors.

So we leave to walk back up the hill in the snow, and sit in the kitchen and drink coffee, while we watch the juncos outside at the feeder, small blue birds with white breasts. Minnesota is Florida for the juncos, who've come down from the Arctic.

We went to Chicago for a wedding, driving down for the reception Sunday night. The bride and groom were old enough to have lots of friends, and they were all happily gathered to eat and talk and raise a glass in good wishes. And she said, our friend the bride, that it's so nice because many of you have been with me through the not-so-happy times.

She's a musician, a singer, so the band started playing early. The first song was a waltz, and she and her husband went out on the floor. A swirl of white and lace and blue and gray and smiles, and the older ladies there, the mothers, said, "He can dance!" Later I'd had a glass of champagne and no one seemed to be paying much attention, so even I went out for a couple of dances, the slow ones, just so I could say I danced with my wife in Chicago.

About ten o'clock the regular band took a break. Some of them went outside to smoke, standing there, sweating, in the snow coming down. And some older friends, some men who'd been over in the corner all night, jazz musicians from Chicago's best years, brought out their instruments. A man with white hair under a black hat sat and strummed an acoustic guitar. A trombone player was soon by his side. And from far back in the corner, the prettiest saxophone music I'd ever heard. Someone said, "Do you know who that is?"

Everyone got quiet and came around, and the man with the black hat and a gruff voice sang to the bride. If it had been in a movie, it would have been too corny. He looked up in her eyes and smiled and sang.

> *When whipporwills call*
> *And evenin' is nigh,*
> *I hurry to my blue heaven.*
> *A turn to the right*
> *A little white light*

*Will lead you to my blue heaven.*
*You'll see a smiling face, a fireplace, a cozy room,*
*A little nest that's nestled where the roses bloom.*
*Just Mollie and me, and Baby makes three.*
*We're happy in my blue heaven.*

Those of us who are lucky, how lucky we are.

24 December

19 degrees

The barometer reading 29.87 and rising

There is full moonlight and the back steps are danger-
ously crunchy and icy, when I go out to read the other
thermometer. We've had ice all week. But you still tend to
forget and walk outside fast, then slip and catch yourself and
gasp and almost pull a muscle. I think of my grandmother
years ago, falling on the ice, walking to church one morning,
breaking an arm, banging up her face. As you get older you
begin to understand that it isn't so much the cold that makes

you think about moving away, moving south, it's the ice, and the fear.

I did fall this week once, but not badly. I was out running with Will, holding his leash. I think he may have pulled me off balance, and I went down backward, an easy landing. I'm there on the sidewalk and the dog comes over, says with a look, "Well, this is a good place to stop."

This has been a difficult time for sleeping, this week, and the reasons involve the light and the darkness and the ice. I'm always restless, it seems, when the full moon approaches, and I spend a lot of time watching the sky.

Wednesday in the late afternoon the moon was rising, and it was luminous, as if you were looking through fogged-up glasses. Then Thursday night the sky was completely overcast, but the full moon was a strong white glow behind the clouds, a light you could sense, outside the house in the night.

It is the time of the solstice, the darkest night of our year. The sun has been rising later, more hesitantly.

That began to change Wednesday, as winter started. Now the days lengthen, and centuries ago this would have been a reason for celebration, the returning of the light. It would have been easy then, early in December long ago, to believe that the world was dying, and to feel each lengthening day as a reprieve.

At night—trying to sleep through all of this—in my dreams or maybe just the thoughts that come in the space between reality and fantasy, I am worried. Worried about tomorrow. Worried about something that happened today.

Thinking of phone calls not returned and of a plane crash in Scotland. Does the Christmas tree have enough water? Does the cat have enough food? And just making up things to be worried about. Like what will I do tomorrow if I can't find a parking place in downtown Minneapolis? I won't find the right present, and then my marriage will be a failure.

If you realize at this point that you'll have trouble sleeping, you can go on down to the kitchen and heat up some milk. Have a cup of warm milk with some honey and just a touch of instant coffee for taste. Sit for a while and turn on the record player, listen to Samuel Barber's *Adagio for Strings*. And then, carefully, make your way upstairs in the dark to bed.

The house is quiet. The bed is still warm, and you know you're sleepy now. Why do I keep thinking about the moonlight and the way it looks on the snow and sparkles on the ice? Why do I think about the quiet cold of the countryside, and the darkness? . . .

An owl calls from high in a tree, there by the edge of the forest. And I move with the wind, along the ice of the river, fast and strong and gliding, one arm tucked behind me, the other one swinging. The long blades of the skates bite into the ice through the dusting of snow. The air rushes past the hood of my racing suit.

The moon is full and warm and empowering; the woods dark and friendly; the small towns peaceful, trusting, with Christmas lights; the church steeples lit in white.

The river runs through the town and under a bridge, and I sweep by fast, a whooshing sound, a child stirs in sleep, dreams of toys and adventure. And I race on, flying on the glistening surface of water, following the river in the dark. At daybreak I'll find a cave to sleep in, and travel again at night.

No one will know I'm there. But maybe I'll stop in the towns and solve problems and rescue people. They'll see me just as I'm disappearing around the bend of the river, a flash of skates, and someone will say, "Who was that?"

In the morning, sitting in the kitchen, strangely tired, I can have a cup of coffee and read the paper and listen to the radio and understand, in the light of day, that the things we worry most about are things that have already happened, or may not happen at all. I'm afraid sometimes that we teach children to do that, that we put the worry there on their faces as they grow older. But I guess we also teach them, especially at this time of year, about joy and being kind and smiling and singing, and about light and darkness.

We went up to the elementary school for a Christmas pageant presented by grade four. We parked out by the street and walked carefully over the ice into the school. There were last-minute giggles coming from the music room. We found the gym and a couple of seats. All the parents were there, and all the brothers and sisters. The lights went down, and spotlights came on.

The fourth grade classmates came out onstage, arranging themselves, grinning. They couldn't help it. Some of the parents waved, started taking pictures. Some of the kids waved, at just about everybody.

You can't look at fifty or so ten-year-olds waiting to sing without grinning yourself. The clothes and the haircuts are just the way they were when you were in school. And you know one child there, in the next to last row, wearing a white shirt and corduroy pants, is going to smile his way through the whole pageant and never sing a word.

The pageant has a fourth grade stage manager and sound effects people and a fourth grade light person. But the light is really coming from the stage to the audience, shining from the energy and pride of the young faces.

And you would like, in a way, to reassure each one: Yes, it becomes more serious, and at times tragic. But always through life, in late December, just about the time of the winter solstice, there will be a moment, every year, that will be almost more than you can stand. Just a thought, a carol on the radio, the face of an old friend, a stranger's smile, a baby's laugh, a moment that will bring a tear and a release of emotion, and you'll know it's Christmas.

31 December

5 degrees

The barometer reading 30.12 and rising

The last quarter moon is in the sky to the south. There must have been a freezing fog in the night, for the trees are shining with ice. Sometimes on mornings like this, chilly and quiet, I'll take a cup of coffee back upstairs. Sometimes my face in the mirror, early, looks like someone else.

It's been stubborn weather here, cold but clear, mostly. The air is dry. The coldest I've been lately was about noon on the day after Christmas, in Indiana, standing around in

snow and thirty-degree weather, and 96 percent humidity—
that's the difference.

We spent most of the day trying to get over to Midway
Airport. We sat on the bus listening to bad traffic news from
the radio, understanding that it would take hours to go forty
miles. When we got to the airport the flight was canceled,
and suddenly we were the people you see on television, in
Chicago, stranded by stormy weather on a holiday. People
sitting on the floor, people lined up to buy bad food, people
saying mean things to one another. But we finally made it
out and safely to Ohio.

We traveled most of the holiday, from one set of parents
to the other and back home. But it was worth it, to hear older
folks laughing and the newest baby crying. We left Indiana
early and didn't have mostaccioli. The recipe is a memory
from Yugoslavia: tomato sauce, onions, ground beef,
chicken. But in Ohio we had more turkey and corn pudding,
and some of the candy that didn't work out well enough to
mail for presents. Fudge, peanut butter fudge, and failed
divinity candy, if there could be such a thing.

My mother's fudge, poured out to cool on a marble slab,
seemed to be the beginning of a week of food nostalgia.
Thursday night I made orange Jell-O and forgot it in the
refrigerator. For lunch the other day I made a grilled cheese
sandwich with tomato soup. Then I went to the store so at
suppertime we could have salmon croquettes.

I found recently in an antique store a shaker made of
aluminum, kind of beaten up but familiar. On the top it said
"Choc-o-malt," and it was the *malt* that I remembered and
had to have and couldn't find in the stores. Finally a friend

brought me a jar from over in Minneapolis, and I put in two teaspoons and filled the shaker, put on the top to shake it up right. It was so fresh and cold, malted milk.

My friends the squirrels outside by the bird feeder, I should report, have been foiled at last. I moved one pole and put a metal baffle on the other, and they can't make the jump. Then I felt guilty and put out a bowl of popcorn on a cold morning, and they loved it. And I got a little curious about how some other animals were getting along, with the below-zero nights, and yesterday went out to the Minnesota Zoo southwest of town.

The Japanese snow monkeys appear quite happy. They are the most northerly of the world's monkeys. Out along the trail in the woods, three Asian lions are sitting in the snow, their coats the color of the oak leaves still on the trees. And Siberian tigers, gold with black stripes. Left to live where they want to, they could be happy at thirteen thousand feet and fifty below. One of the tigers weighs 375 pounds. You wonder how the zoo designers figured out how high to make the fences and if they were good at their jobs.

There's a moose on a hillside, munching. I go by the camels, Bactrian, two humps, shaggy, the Asiatic horses, and then some American elk, seven or so pronghorn antelope, and some bison sitting like large brown rocks on the snow, their breath steaming. The elk, the pronghorns, and the bison once had free range in the grasslands of the West, millions of them.

The zoo's monorail comes gliding by overhead, six white cars with a blue stripe on the side. And I am surprised by a wolf, close by a fence, a wolf watching me. It's large and handsome, and there's nothing scary about it on a sunny afternoon. According to a sign, wolves are now limited to 1 percent of their original range. The sign also says, "What does the word predator mean to you?" and then explains that the two most significant predators to emerge from the Ice Age are wolves and humans. What could the wolves think about the fence? Could the monorail be an exhibit of us for them? Put new people in the cars, have the train go by every twenty minutes?

I've been thinking this way, this week, probably because of a book I've been reading, a book about time and how fast it can go and how delicate our situation in the universe really is. And how things could change, quickly. What if, I've thought, rain came in colors? What if distances got longer as the temperatures got colder? What if people spoke in musical notes?

I can remember one time, when I was maybe ten or eleven years old, quite enthusiastically explaining to my mother a theory I had developed, that I was the only person in the whole world who actually existed. My bedroom would be there when I was looking at it, and the backyard outside the window, but everything else—the school, my friends, my family—would be folded up and put on shelves until the moment I chose to look. This idea made my mother very sad.

The book I've been reading is by the British scientist Stephen Hawking, *A Brief History of Time.* I first looked at his concluding chapter and was relieved to see this sentence: "The question remains, how or why were the laws and the initial state of the universe chosen?"

The state of the universe is the concern of Hawking's

book, and he believes there could be a contracting phase of the universe as well as an expanding phase. In the contracting phase time would run backward. A spilled cup of coffee would put itself back together, fill with hot coffee, and lift back up off the floor onto the table. Or to put it another way, we would die before we were born. But Hawking says that in such a recollapsing universe, with time running backward, there would be complete disorder, and thus intelligent life could not exist.

I remember when I first noticed that I was getting older. I had taken a nap in the afternoon, and when I got up I looked at my face in the mirror. I could see a crease on my cheek, left by a wrinkle in the bedspread. It was there for quite a while.

Maybe it's the mirrors that get you in trouble. Although if I'm careful, standing there, I can still find the right light, and the right expression for my face, and the last ten years are gone. But some days I can see fifty. We are only here for a moment. But it's New Year's Eve, I'm not going to worry about it tonight.

It's warming, but I've been hoping for snow. We had three or so inches this week, but the cross-country ski trains are just barely in good shape. I'd like to get out soon after a couple of weeks of not being all that wintertime healthy.

I've been reading a lot, and eating cheese and crackers, and making plans for soup. Robert Louis Stevenson said, "Many's the night I dreamed of cheese, toasted mostly." One of my favorite cookbooks is full of quotations. The book is by Susan Branch, called *Heart of the Home,* and it offers these words by Louis DeGouy about soup: "It breathes reassurance, it offers consolation."

On a sunny, ten-degree afternoon Will and I go down for a walk along the beach. The Saint Croix River's history flows from the north in Wisconsin and Minnesota. It was the river of the Chippewa, and then the waterway for the great white pine forests, cut down to build the West.

The dog is happy, off the leash, prancing with pride through the snow. It's quiet today, a soft wind high in the branches of the trees, a few birds, and a faint sound of water, moving. The river is frozen quite securely, but along the edge there's usually a couple of feet of clear open water.

I hope the birds know about it. I've been made to feel guilty by warnings. That birds need help in the winter finding water. That you should hook up a small heater in the birdbath or arrange something that would drip, and keep the ice from forming.

I'm thinking about basketball as I walk along, and the death of Pete Maravich. He collapsed on the court during a game with friends. Maravich, forty years old, as good a basketball player as you've seen, died playing basketball. There was mention of trouble with alcohol in the past, but the autopsy produced only wondering. His heart was abnormal, lacking the arterial system on the left side. The doctors said, how could he have run up and down the court like that for twenty years?

And I think of a rainy evening out in the alley back home. I always tried to play basketball, and once, just once, I made a perfect shot, a turnaround jump shot, and I understood the feeling that Maravich had hundreds of thousands of times.

We come back to the house, and try splitting some firewood once again. I have the tool but not the technique; I am clumsy with a splitting maul. I have seen it done correctly, with a dancer's grace and an athlete's timing. There is a danger to it also, and I am usually quite satisfied with a few armloads of wood to carry in.

It's a pleasing fireplace, pale red brick, and built up off the floor so the fire is at rocking chair height. The dog would rather have it closer to his nose. His first winter, three years ago, we lived in an apartment, and his fireplace was a space heater.

This is our first time with birch wood to burn. We use oak and elm for a serious fire, but the birch is light and nice to handle. You can sit and peel the bark off, saving it for kindling.

There is always something new about every fire. You sit and watch, and soon it's like the first time you've ever seen wood burn. There is no learning experience. Even in conversation around a fire, it's okay if your eye is drawn away from your friends and into the dark and the flames. The molecules of hydrogen, carbon, oxygen, become incandescent. It is life—dancing.

You want to find the right music, Mozart, for the snow outside. And you want to make the right soup—your choice. Mine was potato and leek. And you want to find a small poem to salute the fire.

Edna St. Vincent Millay was snowed in once for four weeks in New York State. And she said it was "five miles on snowshoes . . . to fetch the mail or to post a letter. And the thermometer at zero again this morning. . . . All the old

beams and boards that were no good for anything else have
been sawn up and stacked in the most beautiful woodpile
you ever saw.

> *Pile high the hickory and the light*
> *Log of chestnut struck by the blight,*
> *Welcome–in the winter night."*

That's from a book, *Clifton Fadiman's Fireside Reader*,
found, delightfully, one day for fifty cents.

You can tell in the morning that it's been snowing. It's quiet, still. The snow's melting a bit, and blowing in the dark with the wind. The poet A. R. Ammons wrote once about "Snow Ghosts" who "stand up and walk off the roof."

The snow is a blessing to the countryside. In town it's troublesome. In the northern Midwest cities, when it snows the hills are alive with the sound of snow throwers. And I've heard of plenty of folks happy at least to justify somewhat their purchase of two years ago. There's not been much snow.

It does take some work, in town. An alley in Saint Paul can be more of a problem than our country road. This snow came on time, starting in the early evening. Eight or nine inches later, by sunrise, the road was clear for the school bus, our driveway had been plowed, and the newspaper was waiting.

Driving's okay. You have to be careful. I saw a few cars between the lanes of the interstate, but the only one I saw actually stuck was a four-wheel drive, super-equipped vehicle that had been perhaps showing off.

On Sunday and Monday before the snow, in the mornings, the bare tree limbs and the evergreens and the dried grasses were all encased in ice. Bright and clear ice reflecting the low winter sun, then in the shade, appearing white, frosted.

This is hoarfrost ice that would *sound* tinkling. The moisture in the air settles, freezes, to bring the day that you bought your camera for. It is almost as pretty as my favorite wintertime sight, the reflection of light from the snow, either sunlight from low in the west or moonlight. And you don't want to take pictures, they wouldn't be as good.

These days I think often of the light Jim Okonek sees, in the spring and summertime. Jim's a bush pilot in Alaska, really a glacier pilot, flying climbers and sightseers out of Talkeetna to land on the Kahiltna Glacier, 7,200 feet high on the side of Mount McKinley. His world is sunlight on snow, starlight on snow too. Jim Okonek told me he's ener-

gized by the light of the Alaskan summer. Flies eighteen
hours a day. But then in the winter, in the dark, he's sleepy;
it's all he can do to make it over to the couch in front of the
fire after supper at five o'clock.

At our house, two days after the snow, the oil truck came
by. The driver brought the long red hose down to the house
to fill the tank underground. I had never seen this done, so
I went outside to talk. A few hundred gallons went by. Too
much, he estimated.

"You burning the fireplace?"

"Yes."

"Throw off much heat?"

"Not really."

"That's what it is, then, all your furnace heat's goin' up
the chimney."

If he's right, it seems a shame that it should cost you twice
to have a fire going.

After the truck left, Will and I went down to the river,
and far out onto the ice. Dogs walk differently on ice, even
if it's covered by snow. They're thinking about it some. This
is the Lower Saint Croix Scenic Waterway, Minnesota on
one side, Wisconsin on the other. In some places you can
drive from state to state now without benefit of bridge. The
ice, they say, is a foot thick, two it is hoped. And up and
down the river you'll see cars and trucks and fishing shanties
out on the ice.

You tend to think, if you've lived only in a warmer place,
that there's somehow something not right about a river being
frozen over, that there's something wrong because of the ice.
But the river frozen is as natural as the river flowing. Ice

made this country. The glaciers carved the lakes, leaving the soil. Even now glaciers cover 10 percent of the land surface of the earth.

The other night in one of the small river towns, we saw two boys skating. An ice rink had been flooded and frozen in the park. No lights were on; they were just skating, together, in the dark.

When the cold weather came, I began thinking how lucky we are really, as humans and animals, that this planet has such a narrow range of temperatures. One hundred degrees above zero, fifty below. We just put on or take off a few layers of clothing.

Then, within that range, we become amazingly stubborn about our comfort. By exact degrees, we're either comfortable or hot, chilly or not. And almost frightened to think that the man with the oil truck might not come by when the supply is low and the temperature heading down. Think of the deer, curled up in the woods. Think of how the Indians lived.

I'm happy with the weather. But I'll be happy when the spring comes too, so they will quit saying to me, "Well, you haven't been through a Minnesota winter yet."

The day finds moonlight still in the sky. The wolf moon has been bright, disturbing a night of sleep Monday when it was full. I'm glad to be coming into town to the theater, to have an excuse not to go running.

The other day I went out around two o'clock in the afternoon, in sunshine but a pretty good breeze and five degrees above. I was wearing wool socks, blue tights, purple wind pants, a black nylon windbreaker, and a thick layer of Vaseline on my face. With my hood pulled tight, I could hear my breath inside. After half a mile I sounded as though I were about to say something menacing to Princess Leia. There's almost an inch of snow blowing around the icy roads. I love the way the air feels, going into my lungs. But when a car goes past I can taste gasoline, like drops on my tongue.

I've been doing better running than skiing so far this winter, just in terms of staying in shape. Something has happened to cross-country skiing: they've started *skating* on skis. It's a motion similar to ice-skating. It makes the skiing much faster, and it's actually great to watch. But the thing is, I've finally just now learned how to do it the other way, and it feels pretty good striding along until the ten-year-old kids come zipping by, skating past me fast, going uphill.

Although I do recognize this as an opportunity to buy new skis. It was Henry David Thoreau, was it not, who said, "No endeavor is worth undertaking unless it involves buying a whole bunch of new stuff."

Out on the road running I manage a couple of miles or so and get to feeling pretty good and come back in. The dog and cat are waiting. They've been curious about the weather.

The house is just now warming up. There's been no heat all night. The repairman and I were down in the basement this morning talking about furnaces, and he fixed it, although he did have to go into town once for a part. When I work on things, I always like to go into town, too.

We had come home the night before to a cold house, but we keep the thermostat low and it was a while before I noticed. I was cooking, and the olive oil in a cabinet along an outside wall was frozen.

I checked the temperature: it was fifty, and the furnace was quiet. I went downstairs with a flashlight. Fuses okay; oh, there's a reset button on the furnace. I push it and a comforting noise starts up, and I kind of swagger back upstairs. It was nothing, dear. The furnace was out, I fixed it.

As I finished cooking, country-fried steak and leeks, braised in the olive oil, the furnace stopped again. The temperature that night inside the house went down to forty.

So it was early to bed with lots of covers, and Will thought he ought to be up on the bed, to help keep us warm and protect against marauders.

It's a cozy house, but the next morning the furnace man tells me some awful stories about the heat going off and pipes bursting and flooding in the night and older people not being able to get help.

We are just getting through the coldest time of the year, and I start looking up the records: −55 at Warroad, Minnesota, 21 January 1888; −59 at Leech Lake, Minnesota, 9 February 1899. If you think of temperatures as being voices in a choir, imagine the basso profundo of −79 at Prospect Creek, Alaska. Or −81 at Snag in the Yukon Territory. And then try to think of what note would be sounded by the reading at Vostok, in Antarctica, 127 below.

This information comes from a book by Jim Gilbert called *Through Minnesota's Seasons.* It is a book of phenology, the study of natural events that recur periodically. Some reassuring examples: The red oak leaves should start to fall soon—a sign of spring. Some migrant birds—the horned larks and eastern bluebirds—are returning. The raccoons are close to getting out and into the garbage again. At about this week in the far north of Minnesota, black bear cubs are being born to mothers still in winter dens. And this is mating time for the timber wolves. About twelve thousand wolves thrive in the state, mostly in the north. It has been their cold wolf moon.

Here's a final citation of phenology, not from Jim Gilbert but from the sports pages. A truck left Minneapolis this week, going south, an equipment truck carrying baseball equipment belonging to the Minnesota Twins, heading for spring training, and probably the driver stopped for gas, maybe down in Iowa, and heard these warming words from the fellow at the gas station: "How about those Twins?"

On Thursday it was twenty-seven below by the thermometer just outside the kitchen window. In town, on the radio, only thirteen below.

We had a good snow on Monday, five or so inches, a fresh canvas for the immediate natural history of the area. You can see where the deer come down out of the woods at night, past sleeping people in bedrooms, to go on to the river to the open water there along the edge. We saw a fox last week that may have been at the river, a red fox running with speed and power across the field, stopping once to look back.

That cold morning I wanted to find lots to do inside, trying to get some chores out of the way. And I had to find a mouse. I last saw it on a shelf in the bedroom closet, but I didn't say anything because it was late at night, and I knew who would have to deal with it. But now it was time to go hunting. Music helps keep this from being like a scene in a horror film, as I creep down the hallway, stalking the mouse.

I play some old songs by the Byrds, and listen to Jane Siberry and Ry Cooder, Peter Rowan. And James Taylor has a new album with finally a nice rock and roll record title, *Never Die Young.* It reminds me of a scene in the movie *Cocoon*. Wilford Brimley is about to go away to another planet, and he is trying to explain this to his grandson. He says, "Me and grandma are going away, David. When we get where we're going, we won't get any older and we won't ever die." David says, "You're jokin' me, right?"

One of the James Taylor songs is about Valentine's Day, and after listening to just a verse I am back in grade school. We all passed out homemade valentines in the classroom, but I was more deeply involved. Her name was Martha Jane and she was a little plump, but she was really pretty and we were all just a little funny looking in some way then, if you'll remember.

I bought a real valentine with an envelope at a drugstore downtown, signed my name and wrote her name on the front, and then could not mail it and could not take it by her house and finally tore it up and left the pieces between some stones near the tennis courts in the park. Her house was right across the street.

I spent a lot of time there in the summer, playing tennis and hanging around. They were clay courts, and on hot days you could have a dusty drink of water out of an empty tennis ball can. Or if you had a nickle, you could have a Coke. Professor Ross, who ran the courts, would take your money and find you a nice cold bottle back in the case.

Some years later I was in a taxicab, in the summer, going past the park. There was another passenger, a businessman from Chicago. And he said, "Look at that black man teaching that girl to play tennis!" But black was not the word he used, and it wasn't a friendly tone. And I said, "But that's Professor Ross."

I think it's possible that we have these scenes running in our minds all the time, scenes and songs and movies, like a computer's random access memory. There's a story about a conductor who was rehearsing a symphony by listening to it only in his mind. The phone rang; he had a ten-minute conversation with a friend. When he thought again of the music, the symphony had continued to play. It was ten minutes farther along.

When I take a nap in the afternoon now, I often wake up feeling sad, and thinking about a poem Donald Justice wrote:

> *Men at forty*
> *learn to close softly*
> *the doors to rooms they will not be coming back to*
>
> *At rest on a stair landing, they feel it moving*
> *beneath them now like the deck of a ship,*
> *though the swell is gentle*

*And deep in mirrors they rediscover*
*the face of the boy*
*as he practices tying his father's tie*
*there in secret*
*and the face of that father*
*still warm with the mystery of lather*

*They are more fathers than sons themselves now.*
*Something is filling them.*
*Something that is like the twilight sound of the*
  *crickets,*
*immense,*
*filling the woods of the slope behind their*
  *mortgaged houses.*

I think the hope is, don't you, that as we get older, life becomes simpler, that the pleasant thoughts come more easily, that we'll be less afraid, less worried, more willing to love.

In the meantime, that mouse is certainly happy, tucked away in the closet along with the clean towels.

The wind has been up overnight, from the south, with gusts as high as thirty miles an hour.

Earlier in the week we had great days for cross-country skiing, and we went to a state park that once had been woodland and farms. Much of the area was settled by Scandinavians. Nordic skiing *began* in their part of the world. Some brought skis to the Saint Croix River Valley, some even may have skied on these trails, the skiing then being not for recreation but to get from place to place.

Then on Tuesday it turned kind of splashy out near the river. For a couple of days there was icicle rain, with temperatures just around forty. The first night above twenty in a long time. We opened the bedroom window and heard the air rushing, and dogs barking far away again. Will does not like the fresh air that much if it's cold, and then too, he has to pay more attention with the window open. At about 3:00 A.M. something terrible passed by, outside there in the night, and he saved us, with a lot of barking and commotion.

The dog always seems to be on my side of the bed. When he was a puppy, three years ago, I would be sleeping lightly early in the morning. I was quitting smoking then and would be barely asleep. He was just weeks old and wide awake at first light, trying to wake me up, saying, "Get up, get up. Let's go have a cigarette."

We noticed the mailman out on our road this week, leaning to the right driving his car, and I remembered the first time I smoked a cigarette. My father was a mailman and he almost saw me. I had a paper route—we called it "passing papers"—before school.

One dark February morning I went down to the train station, open all night, bought a package of, I think, Lucky Strikes. I had some matches. I walked about five blocks; in the cold on the front porch of an apartment building, I lit a cigarette, and looked down the street and saw my father going in early to work. That was the first one. I remember the last one too.

There was a letter in the mailbox this week from Kentucky, from a friend—a letter written with a fountain pen, answering a question from about ten days ago. I'm pleased by the pace of the discussion. And I understand again how much I don't like talking on the telephone. Years ago in London, it is said, you could correspond with someone across the city in the same day—the postal service was so fast, with so many deliveries in a day, that you could ask a question by post in the morning and have your answer back after lunch.

There was also a note in our mailbox from a neighbor, with some advice to start paying attention to the trees. The buds on the trees, she said, would soon start to get bigger. And they did seem different. Perhaps, on this warm and wet day, the winter could have left?

I've read that already ice-skating on the lakes could be dangerous. Because at the middle of February the sun's light is higher from the sky, more intense, making the ice less reliable. The declination of the sun is thirty-two degrees now, in January it was twenty-four. Also people who keep track of such things would not be surprised to hear that the first crocus has broken through the snow.

The winter may have lost its crunch, but there's no spring green, no purple, no flash of yellow or orange to be seen as yet. We have grays and browns and somber evergreen, the white and black birch trees standing, crookedly, in holes in the snow, which is melting. I make a few snowballs to throw up in the air to the dog, who tries to catch them as he does his tennis ball. But the snowballs go away when he catches them, and he can't find them on the ground.

It isn't fair, so I stop and we come back to the house. I'm determined to bake some bread; I haven't taken the time in a couple of years. In trying to decide on a recipe, I find vegetable names, and the summer comes back fast: cauliflower salad, watercress soup, fresh green peas and tomatoes and peppers and squash. I realize I'm missing our garden at our old house in the East, and the reassurance through the winter of growing onions and lettuce, planted back in October.

The bread, as it turns out, isn't wonderful. But still I present it with pride later in the evening, warm and fragrant. And I am reminded of the night Sally brought us a live mouse, squirming in her mouth. She was pleased with herself and managed a muffled meow, but then she dropped it. It went under the refrigerator. This is the same mouse I couldn't find last week. I hope.

While the bread was baking—it was close to sundown, getting colder, the wind coming up—I had a chore I'd been saving. I wanted to put up a snow fence, out by the garage, to keep the walkway clear. I managed to get the fence unrolled and standing up and fastened okay, thinking yes, indeed, snow I hope. Lots more for skiing, and that means March and April, even May. But you can't have everything you want at the same time.

Close by to where the snow fence now ends, by the garage, standing defiantly there in what will be a bed of flowers, is a sign, brought from another garden, white lettering on black metal. Here's what it says:

> *The kiss of the sun for pardon*
> *The song of the birds for mirth*
> *One is nearer God's heart in a garden*
> *Than anywhere else on earth.*

The winter was over last week.

You can tell by the light. Even on a morning when the temperature is still below zero, the sun is faster and stronger coming over the ridge. And the birds have long been up and about. A lot of new birds, happy and noisy, are out in the trees reporting on what it was like down south.

The newspaper, coming out on Thursday, reports that robins have been sighted already, even a flock of them in a front yard eating frozen berries. I haven't seen one, though

I can recognize robins. I'm having trouble with the rest of the birds.

In the handbook I have, in the index, there's no listing for "little brown ones." One morning we had thirty-five of those, close by the feeder. I did get to know, last year, the red-winged blackbird. And this week I saw an eagle, high in a tree alongside a road. I was driving fast and surprised myself when I saw it. It was mostly white and gray and black, just like the rest of the countryside. It flew away when I stopped, to a higher and more distant tree.

I had been out to visit a cemetery, one that I'd read about and wanted to see, an old cemetery, no longer used, a cemetery in cold snow at the top of the highest hill above town, with the valley of the Saint Croix River below. The caskets would have come up here on wagons drawn by horses.

In a way, these were thankful communities then. The dying passed away among their families and friends, not out in the territories on isolated farms. These were people living together by the river to become merchants, surveyors, rivermen, lawyers, and cabinet makers.

Their town would be built, not ever to be grand but to be their town. A main street, schools, a courthouse, a library, the present one built in 1903. I stopped by to find out some more about the cemetery. The history room was in the basement by the children's room, and the children had come for story hour. I had forgotten how thrilling story hour can be. The children wanted to talk and take a long time getting their coats on, and their gloves and hats, before they left with their mothers.

The cemetery dates from 1850. Today the snow is two

weeks old, but still deep, drifted, the snow of farmland and forest. There are perhaps seventy graves.

*William and Pamela Martin*
*O. D. Ware*

Snowmobiles have been close by here, and a small airplane snarls overhead.

*Stanley Wallin, 1911, born 1901*
*Sophia Weatherby, born August 3, 1929*

The limestone grave markers are softer now by a century. Some of the names are obscured, some of the headstones broken, leaning against trees.

*James Montgomery Fulton, born 1812*
*Jane Clements Fulton, born 1813*

It is bright sunshine and very cold, here among people who have left no other record to history.

*Major Otil Hoyt, Surgeon 1st Massachusetts*
*Infantry*
*Lieutenant Charles O. Hoyt, 38th Wisconsin*
*Infantry*
*Caleb, 1 year, 2 months, 17 days*
*Lizzie, 2 years, 9 months, 20 days*

There are paths in the snow; others have been here, and lots of animals.

*Eleanor Margaret Boyd, died November 12, 1888*
*Mary Parker Savage, 1828–1907*
*Caroline, Wife of John T. Skeffington, 1821–1927*
*Seeley*
*Sturtevant*
*McCay*
*Martlett*
*Durand*

A sign out by the road says, "No artificial flowers May 1st–October 1st."

I have put some Cajun music on in the car on the way home, and also have it playing while I'm cooking some chili. I wonder about graveyards. I know each moment of my visit will remain clear in my memory. I don't know anyone who is not superstitious. Those who say they aren't can be caught doing some pretty strange things around World Series time.

I have trouble leaving rooms. I want to go back and touch something, before it's right to leave the room or the house. I have to walk back over and touch the arm of a rocking chair, or touch a bedside table in a certain place. I've never tried to explain this to my wife, but I know she's noticed. She thinks I'm having an affair with an invisible woman.

Bruce Chatwin, who has written of Patagonia and east Africa, among other places, spent a great deal of time in central Australia with the aboriginal people for his newest book, *The Songlines.* The aboriginals believe their history is recorded as *music* in their memories, "invisible pathways" along and within the country of their ancestors.

The Saint Croix River Valley is inscribed in memory.

The glaciers made the land. The Chippewa and Dakota traveled the river. The pioneers, moving west, stayed and built their lives and graveyards. The robins, by instinct, know the way north and back to the valley.

This day, this sunshine in late winter, has been seen before.

There is quite a lot of snow on the ground, fluffy and wet. This is the snow that comes, they say, at state hockey tournament time, in Saint Paul.

This snowstorm was well tracked coming over the Rockies, with thunderstorms out front and lightning and sleet. The warnings were out two days ago. It was a warm week, and earlier we had some rain—a nightful of it—the first water falling from the sky since back in November. Open the door in the dark. Listen. And breathe the cool and wet, now springtime, air.

The snow will be gone quickly. The ice on the Saint Croix River looks rotten and risky, although I saw some people out fishing on Thursday, just standing there on the ice, looking stubborn.

The smell of manure is in the air, from the fields nearby, melting. One day the dog and I got close enough to another smell, on the road by a field. A large skunk was eating something. I stopped the car—I could have caught it if I'd wanted to, the dog definitely wanted to. The skunk didn't run. It sort of scuttled across the field as if its back were broken. I realized I'd never seen a live skunk before. We see them dead, when they don't scuttle fast enough. And we see them in cartoons.

Will was disappointed when the skunk left. He was already somewhat disgruntled because it was the day to go to the vet's for a heartworm check. It's just a blood test, he was fine. But he doesn't like to go, and he knows what's happening because of the way I talk to him in the car. I am, of course, guilty in these moments of anthropomorphizing this dog. But of my shortcomings, that worries me the least.

After the visit to the vet and a stop for lunch, I drive out in the country a ways to an animal shelter. We would have called it, growing up, the dog pound. This is a good one, carefully run mostly by volunteers. I pull into the parking lot, leave Will in the car, and listen to the barking. Today it is less frantic, just playful.

In the building the dogs come up close to you, against the wire of their kennels. They might bark at first, but what they really want is to be touched, to be talked to.

— A dog named Honey, Newfoundland-collie mix, found on highway, hold for five days.

Even the dogs that are strays, with no collar, now have names. Someone does that for them.

— A border collie named Susie, one year old, housebroken, friendly, $42.50 adoption fee.

There's a $15 refund if you have the dog spayed or neutered.

— Shadow, part huskie, part poodle, very sweet, found, can't keep, housebroken.

Well, wouldn't they all be housebroken? What would you say if you were giving up your dog and they asked you that question at the shelter?

— Charity, a female, black and white, mostly hound, has been abused.
— Candi, golden retriever, $53, good with kids.
— Smokie, a sheltie mix, friendly eyes, a gruff bark, scared, the sign says, "playful, sweet"; reason for surrender, "going into nursing home."

I've seen other reasons: chases, chews, too much trouble, has fleas bad, just don't want.

— Willie, a black Lab mix, nice, friendly, it says, chews, barks, needs someone to care for him.
— Pansy, one year old, Lhasa apso, cream colored, owners are moving away.
— Casey, shy but sweet, a sheltie, child has allergies.
— Spud, a husky and sheltie mix, no one home to care for.

And sleeping, sprawled on the floor on a bed of shredded newspaper—Mico, Murphy, Mac, Max, Mandy—black, brown, and tan, six weeks old, maybe seven, mostly Doberman puppies. The sign says, "Left at shelter in box." Put your hand down over the side of the cage, take them up. Nothing is softer than a puppy.

There's a sign very close to the puppy cages: "If you're not sure, get a fern." There must be thirty-five puppies here today. Far too many, and perhaps half of them must soon be "put down." That's the term at the shelter. Back at the car Will is waiting, without even any jealous sniffing, and we drive home quietly. I think he understands about the shelter. He came from one in Virginia, and I believe he knows that someday we'll get another dog. We come here often.

Here's a quotation I don't agree with: "Brothers and sisters, I bid you beware / of giving your heart to a dog to tear." There can be sadness with dogs but always, also, joy. I didn't have a dog before and didn't realize how funny they are, how much enthusiasm they can bring to a moment.

And if things get rough, it's good to have a dog around.

And we are all of us alike, in a way: the dogs in the shelter, hoping for the confusion to end, and the fear, the skunk out there in the field, trying to find supper, the rest of us just doing our best, trying to get by.

A cold mist is in the air, and some flurries. Most of last week's snow is gone. The Saint Croix River is still frozen over, but with lots of open water, and in some places it has become possible, in theory anyway, again to travel by boat between Minnesota and Wisconsin. We saw an eagle this week, splashing down onto the icy blue river to attack a fish. The eagle lifted away from the water, circling low and then climbing fast.

It was a much nastier day last Sunday over in Saint Paul.

I guess I should report on my efforts in that day's eight-kilometer run, since I was careless enough to mention on the radio that I'd entered. It was a Saint Patrick's race, along an old Victorian avenue, high on a bluff above the Mississippi, then past the cathedral down into the city. The morning came eighteen degrees cold, and windy. I didn't want to get too tired before the race by running around warming up for a half hour. So I started cold and stiff, and ran along sort of daydreaming for about three miles, wondering why I was being passed by people who had obviously eaten, during the winter, many more doughnuts than I had.

I got serious about the speed of this race only when I came to the last mile and realized that I was going to be able to finish, that the last part was all downhill, and that the results—names and times—were going to be in the newspaper the next day. I finished, running faster than I had started, but slower than 2,490 other runners. I took my green T-shirt and left satisfied anyway. I stopped at the supermarket for a reward, where I was tempted by malted milk balls, settled for low-salt Wheat Thins, but then ate most of the box on the way home.

We do try to find youth at springtime. Sometimes, though, it's only to be found in memory. On the interstate the other day, my car was passed by a pale green Chevrolet Deluxe, 1952, I'm certain. A young man was driving, a fifties haircut, his right hand high on the steering wheel, rock and roll surely on the nontransistorized AM radio. He's Neal Cassady in Kerouac's *On the Road*. If you've got a couple of dollars for gas, there's nothing to worry about.

I had a Chevrolet like that once, bought it to drive home

after working for a summer outside of Denver, laying sewer tile. I was going to be a senior in high school and play football and have a car, but it broke down—the motor seized and stopped—in a small town in Kansas. I left the car at a gas station, sold it for fifty dollars. It had been a rainy night, and I was playing the radio loud and didn't notice the rod starting to knock. My father picked me up at the bus station when I got home.

The old green Chevrolet on the road was surely a sign of spring, and I decided to go looking for others. I drove over to the feed store to smell the oats and the shelled corn and the grass seed, and to buy fresh suet balls for the woodpeckers, get them through a couple more months.

Then I went out to a trout stream, pretty far back in the woods. The water flows dark and fast. Along the path April is getting ready. Skunk cabbage and several shades of moss have brightened in the warming air. One patch of moss on a tree stump is such a green it makes me think of leprechauns.

There is a sign by the trout stream: "Open first Saturday in May, 5 am, flies only, one trout 13 inches." The sign does not say, "Be patient, good luck." The fish, German brown trout and rainbow, don't know about the sign. The eagle—high above the Saint Croix River, just downstream—will not wait for May.

26 March

24 degrees

The barometer reading 29.76 and rising

The wind has been alive yesterday and through the night, mostly from the south and west. Steady and strong, twenty, thirty, even sixty miles an hour.

But it was a wind from warmer places, and not threatening, even though it blew grit and knocked over garbage cans and brought tree limbs down. Not threatening, even though we saw smoky black clouds swirling together with white, and heard, on Thursday, the awful wail of the big sirens. The tornado warning system was being tested.

It's state high school basketball tournament time in Saint Paul, and it's somewhat distracting to see all the young players walking around town. I had a thought for a moment that the wind might come gusting along and take me away into the clouds and set me down in a backyard in a small Minnesota town, thirty years younger, ten inches taller.

Out on the river, on the Saint Croix, we are watching the ice as closely now as we did back in November when it was freezing. We are impatient for open water, to be paddling with the wind in a canoe, or drifting with the stream along the shore, to be moving at speeds and with rhythms not of our choosing.

It was startling to see, the other morning, in the light just before sunrise—gray and blue light the same color as the ice—a cross-country skier out on the river, cruising along, double-poling, moving fast with confidence. We couldn't decide if someone would be better off or not with skis on if the ice should happen to crack open.

I've seen now some clothes hanging out to dry, and bales of hay on the back of a slow truck going through town. Our spring, by the calendar, has been here since last Sunday morning, but true spring is still on its way north. We've been buying asparagus, from California, I think, and I remember a story I like to tell about asparagus and springtime in France. It's about asparagus fans who, early every spring, travel down through France to the border of Spain, and then move back north, a few miles a day, through the countryside. They are moving with spring and the asparagus harvest each day. Each day they eat the freshest possible asparagus, with sweet butter and local bread and wine. I've told that story so much I've forgotten if it's true.

Back around 1950 the naturalist Edwin Way Teale published a book called *North with the Spring*. Teale and his wife, Nellie, traveled from Florida to New Hampshire, starting in February. It's a wonderful book about that journey. You learn, for example, that robins move north, all the way to Alaska, moving with the thirty-five-degree isotherm. The migrating robins just stay at thirty-five degrees. And Edwin Teale writes: "Spring advances up the United States at the average rate of about fifteen miles a day. It ascends mountainsides at the rate of about a hundred feet a day. It sweeps ahead like a flood of water, racing down the long valleys in a rising tide. Each year the season advances toward us—out of the south, sweeps around us, goes flooding away into the north."

Some years ago I decided to try to hike the Appalachian Trail by myself, walking from north Georgia to Mount Katahdin in Maine. You do that walk from south to north, moving with spring. I failed quickly, within ten days; didn't get out of Georgia. I realized that I really didn't want to do it, wasn't all that comfortable being uncomfortable in the woods, being alone. Next time I hope to do better.

We're getting close now these days to making friends again with our weather. Soon there's a day, a morning, when you're outside without a jacket, and it's so warm you wouldn't even need clothes. The air around you feels as if it has no temperature. It is the wind of tornadoes, but it is also the breeze of springtime gentleness.

I think often of the creatures in Tolkien's *Lord of the Rings,* the hobbits especially, traveling through the woods, sleeping under the trees, fearful of the weather and of what might be alive under the ground. Our world can be dangerous, but usually with warning. It is not the night that will hurt you.

9 April

44 degrees

The barometer read 30.33 and rising

The weather radio mentions snow. There's a good wind and gray daylight, and birds talking out in the trees. Some of them are just passing through, moving north. There's been a lovely bird at the feeder, brown with a breast the color of lemon sherbert. May be a yellow warbler, may in fact be several birds—there's a whole category in my guidebook called "Confusing Fall Warblers."

We've had sea gulls around for about seven days now, down by the water. And that could be why they're here, arriving as the ice leaves. But do you notice how humans are always trying to figure out what sea gulls are doing so far inland, so far away from the sea? It's as if we think they've got it wrong.

The ice left in a week's time. It did not "break up," but that's what the neighbors called it when they talked about who won the money in the pool this year. The ice just melted and left, moving out away from the shore. I guess Thursday would have been the official day, even though that afternoon I saw big sheets of ice, sea gulls standing on top, drifting with the river and the wind.

I have been for walks through the warm dry air of spring, finding snowdrops in the woods, the flowers of winter's end, white and surprising green against the dry leaves on the ground. I've watched the sky for eagles. One showed itself, low, by the river this week. And I've stood at dusk on the ridge, looking at the young birch trees. The white of the birch in the late light is the same as in the mist of sunrise, a luminescent white. If I were a painter, this is where I would come, in secret, and try to capture that light.

A week or so ago we went east for a couple of days to see some friends and to check on the daffodils and forsythia we had planted in our old garden by our old house. I had forgotten about forsythia's bold, happy yellow. The cherry trees were almost in bloom, and out in the countryside of Virginia, where the streams come down off the mountains, the spring peepers were out and loud, insisting.

When we came back to the Twin Cities, driving in from the airport, the streets seemed deserted, the sidewalks empty. It's only by comparison with the eastern cities that you will notice this. It's like a science fiction movie at first.

I guess, though, the springtime I had been waiting for was found out on the open water of the Saint Croix, after four months of ice. On a windy morning, the sun still behind the ridge, I put on boots, a hat, life jacket, gloves, take the paddle, leave the dog behind, lay the boat in the water, step out and in—a balance remembered. And the canoe moves out from the shore, gliding, rocking, just a little. The water answers the paddle, and the world is different. Paddle once on one side, then the other. You are on the same level as the ducks and the sea gulls, and they have noticed. Turn the bow into the wind and pull hard, then let the boat coast.

In the *Atlantic* magazine this month, there's an article—it's the cover story—entitled "Did the Universe Just Happen?" Robert Wright, the author, tells the story of Edward Fredkin, a scientist who believes that the universe is a computer. Not that the universe operates *as if* it were a computer, but *is* a computer. That all the universe's electrons and atoms are ultimately bits of information moving inside a computer—a computer that is in the process of working on a problem.

The idea is one of digital physics. The genetic instructions contained in DNA would be a good example of digitally encoded information. Fredkin says his "universe as computer" is designed by intelligence, and is being used by somebody or something. Kurt Vonnegut did this to us once in a book, had our galaxy exist only so that a spare part could be delivered at a certain time to a faraway planet. But Vonnegut writes fiction.

Edward Fredkin is an admired theorist, even if not all of

his colleagues actually agree with this idea. I do recall talking with a physicist once in Cambridge who was pretty sure that in the future brains would be kept alive to become organic computers. A human brain, on a shelf, with wires attached, available on command.

I think about all this in the canoe, perhaps wasting time. The day is coming up fast with the sun, and this is one of those imponderables I don't much like to fool with before breakfast. I wonder if Edward Fredkin has ever been out early on the river, but then maybe it would only prove some of his points. Maybe all of this could have been done only by computer design.

The way the wind moves the water; the infinite shades of blue and gray and white when the river was frozen; a feather, falling from the sky.

Perhaps, though, all of these things absolutely *disprove* the theory. I'll put the canoe away and go for coffee, and talk to the dog. He might make more sense. But if the universe is a computer, I sure would like to know what problem it's working on.

Just going by the calendar, it will not be long now before we can report the sight or sound of painted turtles, eastern bluebirds, purple martins, common snipe, red maple trees in bloom, trillium, lilies of the valley, wood ticks, smelt, asparagus.

Hal Borland, the author of hundreds of nature editorials for the *New York Times*, said that in April, "miracles . . . happen every day before sundown. Nothing is newer than an April morning, nothing more full of wonders than a bud or a seed. April is . . . a tired, disillusioned world of frost and ice and snow made innocent once more. It is a tempered wind and a warming rain, and almost fourteen hours of daylight."

In our front yard we found a long, fat night crawler, and we heard a frog this week, up in the woods. I've finally seen a couple of robins, and one morning a pair of ducks—the female spotted brown, the male green, gray, and chestnut— came striding into the yard, looking for a nesting site.

They left soon. It wouldn't have worked. Our dog would have been far too friendly a neighbor, always snuffling and sniffing around. "Let's go play. You run, I'll catch you."

We were out in the canoe on Monday. The water was flat at noon, fifty degrees but warm. It was the first good two-hour paddle, the river between seasons and empty of ice and boats. Along the shore coming back, a Canada goose started honking, loudly, making a lot of noise so we wouldn't notice his mate over there by the trees on her nest. And in the woods last fall, we were startled by a grouse running along the ground, pretending to have a damaged wing, trying to lead us away from a nest.

This week out in the country, along the roads, I saw tractors for sale, shined up, greased, and ready to go. And I sat drinking coffee at a restaurant, reading the paper, trying not to listen. "Are you gonna do any carpenter work?" "Only my regular customers." "We buried my father last week." "Dry, isn't it?" "Gonna be a dry summer; gonna be like Africa here."

There are lots of comings and going in the small town, and I found my excuse to go into the grain elevator and the feed store. It is time for some onion sets, a couple of pounds of thistle for the bird feeder, a check on dog food prices. It would help if I had a pickup truck so I could just back it up there to the dock.

Then I chanced on a conversation about bluebird houses. A woman came into the store and asked if anyone had seen a bluebird. The man behind the counter, with a wink in his voice, said they'd be coming through the valley next Thursday at one o'clock; just put the bluebird house up about five or six feet high. You should have several, make what they call a bluebird trail, by the edge of an open field.

There are also boats for sale, sitting in front yards, with red and white signs taped to the windshields. If you could buy, this spring, something big like that, what would it be? A tractor, an old pickup truck, a speedboat? You'll have more friends with a boat. You'll get more work done with a tractor. With a truck, about all you'll do is go into town to get stuff.

I imagine a truck for myself sometimes. It's an old Ford, black, maybe a short bed, 289 V-8, a soft rumble in the morning before light. Wipe the dew off the windshield, put the thermos on the seat, let the radio warm up. I think of that truck this week while walking at dusk, looking at the different trees and bushes, their blossoms and buds. Life—green and fresh and damp—coming once more.

Isn't it an aching feeling, springtime? Don't you sometimes wish you could start again?

23 April

34 degrees

The barometer reading 29.65 and rising

A night, finally, of dampness, a chilly and pleasant rain.

I went out to run—just to get some moisture into my body, to breathe the cold, freshened air. Then, as I came back down the road to the house, the raindrops became icy and turned to heavy wet snow falling straight down fast.

We went on a short trip this past weekend, driving along down the Saint Croix River. Twenty miles south it enters the Mississippi. We drove on to a very small town, a very old hotel. In 1864 someone had slept in this room. And the town was silent at night, the river half a mile away.

In the stillness from the north or perhaps the south, it was hard to tell, you'd hear a train whistle. A diesel, moving fast, a gathering, clattering rush, then a roar. The whistle again, booming now as the train racketed through, not slowing, and then was gone around the curve along the river. This happened maybe once an hour, all night.

If you were going to be thinking about ghosts in an old hotel room like this, you wouldn't be really getting yourself too scared before the train would come through to take your mind off of it. This was not a nostalgic whistle. These were working trains, due someplace within hours.

After that night I wanted to *stay* back in the past for a while, to stay in the time of old hotels and towns and trains. And so it was then entirely appropriate that the next day a present was delivered. It was my birthday, and a surprise from my wife. She had found a splendid old radio, a Stromberg-Carlson 1937 chair-side model. Glowing parchment-colored dial, green tuning eye, police band, amateur phone, Geneva, Japan, night aircraft.

On this radio you could have heard William Shirer of CBS reporting on the Nazi invasion of Poland. And someone surely did listen, nightly, as the war continued, and was ended at last. What a fearful and wonderful thing, to be listening to the world then. The death of Roosevelt, a new president, and the fifties began, and *I* could have been listening, to the detective shows and the serials each week.

Our Gal Sunday—"Can a girl from a small mining town in Colorado find happiness with England's richest, most handsome lord?" And baseball—the road games being re-created there in the studio. And on Saturday nights the Opry coming in, fading, over the mountains it seemed from Tennessee.

You may recall John Cheever's short story *The Enormous Radio.* A young couple in Manhattan, Jim and Irene Westcott, decide to buy a magnificent new radio for their living room. The old one had stopped playing one Sunday in the middle of a Schubert quartet. But the new radio doesn't work at first. And then it becomes clear that it doesn't pick up radio stations at all, but instead the Westcotts can hear conversations from other apartments in their building. The Sweeneys in 17-B; the Fullers in 11-E. They could turn the dial and find people snoring, people arguing, people making love.

But then the Westcotts realize that other people can hear *them,* on radios in their own apartments. And the Westcotts haven't been getting along all that well either.

One afternoon this week, putting radio reveries aside, I took the solo canoe out on the river, putting in about three miles downstream from the highway bridge, where Interstate 94 crosses. The wind was up a bit, from the north, but I wanted to see if I could make it to the bridge, and did, about an hour and a half later.

I did have about thirty seconds of panic once, in the wake of a motor boat, my life jacket unzipped, forgetting for the moment that I was in only about three or four feet of water. I'm not always comfortable in a solo canoe. It's so tippy that you can't even turn around to look behind you, or at least I can't.

When I got up close to the bridge, the noise from the traffic got louder, a constant roaring sound. I've heard B-52 bombers taking off from a couple of miles away sounding that way. There were lots of trucks on the bridge, carrying cattle, concrete blocks, furniture, frozen pizza. Lots of cars too. In a canoe from underneath the interstate, you wonder where everyone can be going so fast, on these highways that President Eisenhower wanted built as a matter of national defense. The trucks pass overhead, slamming and booming, and I think the canoe is shaking, as if the shock traveled down the pillars to bedrock and then spread up through the water to the boat.

I leave quickly, slipping out from under the bridge and along the shore. Soon it's quiet again, the sun comes out. I paddle along slowly, not thinking much of anything. A loon appears alongside the canoe, cautious but curious, wondering. And so am I. Wondering if this loon has been up there close by the bridge to look at the cars and trucks. And if so, is it trying to figure out, why would anyone want frozen pizza to be moving so quickly from one place to another?

A few wispy clouds in the early sunlight, white and slate gray and rose, and the water of the river is taking its color from the sky. There's hardly any wind.

It's a balloon morning. They should be out soon. The hot-air balloons float out over the Saint Croix and then rise high above Wisconsin, up near, it seems, where the airplanes are passing close by, descending to the airport twenty miles west. The balloons hang in the sky—red and blue and yellow—four of them, now five. There's one way down

there by the river. They float to the east and south, out of
reach of dogs barking below. And the rest of us go on to
work.

April is a time for impulse, especially in the upper Midwest, where spring takes such a long time resolving itself.
There is not all that much to be responsible about. It is too
early for the garden or to be worrying about the grass. You
find yourself wanting to buy flowers, as a surprise. Or try
a color you've not thought of wearing before. Or drive, just
anywhere. The people in the balloons end up two thousand
feet high on an April whim.

April can be just about as adventuresome as we get. This
week I was kissed by an eighty-two-year-old man. We were
becoming friends, and he was serious about it. He gave me
a present: a white pine tree, thirty-five inches tall, the tree
growing in a pot along with violets, unfurling up from the
dirt.

What *I* did one day was call a fellow I know, who called
somebody else, and we watched the weather the next morning and decided on three o'clock in the afternoon and met
out at the airfield. It's just a grass strip, once part of a
farmer's avocation, now a few hangars and some older re-
built light aircraft and four or five gliders, sailplanes. It is
my intention to go up in one of these gliders, one that
belongs to a local soaring club.

It's a teaching craft, eighteen feet long, aluminum, white
with yellow trim, and two seats—the instructor sits in back
and talks reassuringly.

Chuck is old enough for this. He's retired and has flown
more than eight hundred times in gliders. I sit in front,

strapped in, trying not to touch anything. The instruments are explained, a checklist finished. A tow plane comes up, attaches, we bump noisily down the grass and quickly into the air.

The motions of this light craft, taking off under tow, are surprisingly abrupt, with sudden small deflections and corrections. It sort of feels like being inside a large plane, landing in bad weather. We circle, climbing steadily, and then release the cable. The tow plane goes left, we go right, a sharp banking turn. The air whistles in through the vents, the sky is above and around us all at once. There is a lot to watch.

But Chuck is worried about the altimeter. We're dropping fast. There's a plowed field ahead and he angles toward that, calculations running in his mind. The gliding ratio for this plane is: if we were one mile high, we could glide out in a straight line for twenty-eight miles without any extra lift from rising warm air.

Chuck keeps searching for thermals, feels a bump now and then from an air pocket. He tells me he's going to put the plane in a sharper bank if it doesn't bother me. Oh no, I'm fine, I say. We lean over forty-five degrees to the right; my body leans left, although I read later that's not right. You must trust the ship. But haven't you wondered, if you've experienced moments like this, what would happen if all of a sudden the laws of physics stopped working?

Chuck is pretty discouraged, can't find any lift, and we have to turn for a landing. He'd been wanting to give me a chance at the controls, to fly, if only for a moment. I'm fine, I say.

We come in too fast, the angle's too steep, he's made a big mistake! But the landing is perfect, feathery, gliding onto the grass.

We have been to three thousand feet and flown fifteen minutes. The next day I look up some records. Gliders have gone higher than forty thousand feet and stayed aloft for many hours. Chuck is not happy about our flight, but I am. There is a slogan I've read on the wall of a flying club in England: "All aircraft bite fools."

And I'm thinking of this a day or two later while watching a bald eagle get ready for supper. I'm outside a large cage. The eagle is three years old and, to my eye, menacing. It is taking some time selecting white rats, large fat ones, from a food bucket. Two are chosen and pulled out with one foot, grasped in the talons.

The eagle is quite comfortable, in residence at a nature center, south on the Saint Croix. There are hundreds of acres of woodland and pasture, high above the river. There are thousands of birds, it seems, lots of bluebird trails, banding stations for research. And a raptor recovery center; birds of prey that are sick or have been hurt are brought here.

And schoolchildren come every day when it's warm, to learn about the birds, to see up close the eagle, a turkey vulture, a large friendly owl. Owls are great for kids; an owl can turn its head almost all the way around, listening for food moving along the ground.

And a red-tailed hawk. That was my interest, to see the hawks. The sailplane pilots at the airfield had talked of watching for the hawks, then following them up into the thermals, circling ever higher. The hawks, the eagles, all the raptors, fly for hours aloft on the warm air, seemingly motionless, watching.

We have learned the physical rules of flight from these birds. But it was not until last night, out walking after dark, with the moon climbing in the sky from the east, that I realized—there is a difference. Birds are birds; *we* really don't need to fly. It can be exhilarating, it can be convenient. But we would have been all right, I guess, if we'd never figured out how to do it.

A good wind from the southeast ruffles the water of the Saint Croix.

At 6:50 I was already thinking about a nap. I was back from fishing, back from breakfast. A good breakfast, but ordinary, it did not include pan-fried trout. "Don't expect fish," it's been said about opening day. "The first days of trout fishing are like oriental philosophy—more fishing than fish."

This was the opener in Wisconsin. Minnesota starts next

week. I wanted to do some fly-fishing on a small river, close by in Wisconsin, a "special regulations" trout stream that empties eventually into the Saint Croix. I'd been to the stream in late winter. There I found a lot of snow, some ice, but flowing water and much promise, and a sign that dared me to come back, equipped, at 5:00 A.M. on the first Saturday in May.

I have tried to be a fisherman because I like reading about it so much. And a friend in Washington once told me that when you're standing out there in the river with the water up to your chest, it feels as though the world is turning around you. Over a few years I collected some equipment: a fly rod and reel, a vest—full of important small implements—a videotape about casting, which I haven't watched.

This week, in a panic one afternoon, I bought some flies for the waters of western Wisconsin. I was cautious in the store. A beginner cannot take a proper part in the conversation that is customary upon selecting a dozen flies. I didn't want to admit that I had yet to catch my first fish.

My alarm was set for four o'clock this morning. I got out of bed ten minutes after that, and rushed to find the fishing stuff. The rod case was out in the garage. I should have practiced casting some, and tying that special knot that attaches the fly to the tippet on the end of the line.

I have some coffee but decide not to fool with the big thermos. I usually take it everywhere in the early morning. I've had it since twenty years ago, bought it then to take to the job with me, a steel thermos that wouldn't break when it followed you out of the truck and hit the ground.

Driving out to the river, I listen to AM radio. The disc

jockey is talking about recovering from a heart attack; he's feeling fine now, doing well on a stress test, getting used to skim milk and oatmeal. He plays Neil Diamond's song "Sweet Caroline," a song I've always secretly liked.

The windows are down, it's warm outside, ten minutes to five. A few birds have started singing. Today they seem happier. I wish I knew the birds by their song, but I don't even think I would recognize an oriole. These migrant birds have returned now to the upper Midwest from Central America. That is supposed to happen, and did, on May 1st. Last Sunday an oriole was seen, and some people put out orange halves and grape jelly and water to welcome them.

Last week we did, of course, recognize the song of the whipporwill at dusk, in the woods outside the house, the echoing, liquid sounds: *whip-poor-uh-will,* calling, pausing, until an answer comes back in. A lighter voice. Silence, and then the first bird has moved, and the second one too, as the calling moves along the hillside in the dark. There is a spookiness to it, these birds out in the night.

I've been reading a new book by James Kilgo, about his childhood in South Carolina, time spent along the bottomlands of the Pee Dee River. The book is called *Deep Enough for Ivorybills.* And he recalls, "When I was a boy there were men in my hometown who were respected for their knowledge of birds. They were not bird lovers in the usual sense of that term but farmers and foresters who spoke without self-consciousness about such things as declines in the redheaded woodpecker population or the rare occurrence in our area of a painted bunting."

The birds of the Saint Croix River Valley all seem to be

awake now, as I drive along a narrow road at five minutes to five. Lightning has been threatening, and now rain begins lightly on the windshield. The first rain in a long while. The wettest thing for the past ten days or so has been my dog's nose.

There are cars there waiting, and trucks, ten or fifteen of them, at the bridge crossing the trout stream. Men and women are moving about in the dark, collecting equipment, pulling on waders.

I leave the car, grab a flashlight and my fishing gear, and walk quickly upstream, away from most everybody else. They must know I'm going the wrong way. The water sounds friendly. The air is moist and warm, just a few spatters of rain.

I come to the place where, before, I planned to fish: a grassy bank, the stream flowing past some rocks and deeper pools. And I decide not to stay. I decide not to assemble the rod and tie on a fly, not this morning. I've been impatient, rushed, moving too quickly.

It may or may not be right to take a fish from a trout stream, but it is certainly *not* right to do it in a hurry. Opening day will be over. There will be another morning to fish, by myself. I leave quickly, passing others just arriving. I drive to a truckstop for breakfast, read the paper, play rock and roll on the radio going home. But the darkness of that stream stays with me, the dripping of the rain—the promise of the morning. I have not left the river.

It's cold weather. I was wearing a down jacket last night, out walking.

I've been wanting to stay outside as long as possible. There's some light past ten o'clock at night, you can see the sun in the west, perhaps out over Montana. And the nighttime air tells you stories, brings you memories.

It was a Methodist hymn, growing up: "He's the lily of the valley, / The bright and morning star." Those flowers were in the side yard when I was a child, and we have them out by the front porch now. And lilacs are everywhere, especially in the towns. They welcomed us to Minnesota this week in May last year.

Later I read about lilacs in Patricia Hampl's book about growing up in Saint Paul. The book is called *A Romantic Education.* She recalls wanting badly to be a writer in high school, and composing lyrical poetry about her discovery of lilacs:

> [They] had always been there in the back yard, down the neighborhood alleys where they cloaked the garbage cans and hugged the sides of old garages too small for the finned fish of that decade's cars. For the first time the lilacs came to me nostalgically because I *noticed* them. Nostalgia and the living, immediate lilac met in a first sensation of adulthood, the knowledge that objects carry their dense bundles of significance out of unconsciousness all the way to—I could almost sense it ahead—the end of the line. To death.

This week it was also, possibly, the week of morels. It's hard to know if it's the right time to go out in the woods hunting for this said-to-be most wonderful of mushrooms. They grow only for a few days, in secret places. And if you call someone on the phone who should know, he'll say, "Why do you ask? Well, maybe next week."

After many phone calls some sympathy is evoked and a white paper bag arrives with a few morels inside. Not from around here, you understand, these are from Idaho. And they were quite wonderful, fried that night in butter. We also panfried some smelt in honor of the season. The small silvery smelt came from Lake Superior, by way of the supermarket.

I went on a short, exploratory canoe trip this week, leaving the fishing gear at home. I wanted to see a few miles of a river, running through the woods down from a state park, and a dam.

It's a warm day, threatening rain. Put the boat in the water, hold it against the current. I'm wearing tennis shoes, no socks. I've rolled up my pants legs. I settle into the boat, moving off into the middle of the stream.

I follow the line through the first small set of rapids, the water moving just faster than you could walk. The riverbank is above your head. The landscape goes past you in a soft blur, vibrant with full spring. A thousand shades of green, and pinks and whites and yellows. There's a drizzle of blossoms in the air, and a mist of pollen, and swirls of insects flying through it all.

You touch the paddle to the water, a slight adjustment, bring the bow of the boat to the left to miss the tree limb out over the water. But you misjudge it. The top of the canoe catches against the branch, the back of the canoe swings around, lodges against some tree, snags on the other side. And the current then easily turns the boat over, and you're in the water.

The water's cold. The boat fills up. I have to drag it to shore and onto the bank to turn it over. I still have my hat; car keys, I note with pride, are snapped to a belt loop.

I get the boat back into the water and paddle off, faster now. The river turns to the left, I make it around and then sharply to the right. This is like cross-country skiing, downhill, when you come to a curve at the bottom and just go straight on into the snowbank.

There's a hard thump. The stern of the canoe turns downstream. I'm facing east, the river's running west. There is half an oak tree over the water, and the boat crashes into it. And again I wade ashore, with my nifty solo canoe.

This is not dangerous white-water canoeing. This is just a fast, narrow river, happy to be going on its way without me. I don't stop for lunch. I've not brought it; if I had, I would have lost it. And again I start downstream, and it's easier now. The river widens. About a mile passes, it's quiet, no one fishing.

A couple of river cabins are on the bank, small wooden summer cabins painted red. A screened porch, a white chair, a bird feeder, what more would you want? In front of me, on the water, out around each corner, great blue herons clatter up into the air, disturbed.

Then some more rapids, more dead trees. And I hit— sideways this time—hard. The boat goes under, I try to hang on. The water's chest deep; I can't find my glasses; I still have my hat; I think I'm getting mad.

I sit there for a time on the bank of the river and notice that this is a perfect spot. Here is the freshest green grass of the spring and thousands, it seems, of tiny orchids, purple with blue markings. The whole riverbank is covered with them.

I've been in this moment in books. The oak tree is going

to talk. The hobbits and the elves are going to come by and take me off on a quest. I pick just a few of the flowers and put them in my shirt pocket, where it's wet. With resolve, I set off again downriver. And the rest of the trip is uneventful.

The river comes into a lake, and far ahead I can see a bridge, with cars crossing. I move closer to shore, drifting. There's a large birch tree on the bank that branches out over the water. I hear a bird's call—loud, sharp. In the branches there's a nest being built, wispy, white. And then I see perhaps the only bird I could identify at this distance without my glasses—the vivid orange and black northern oriole.

I've seen deer this week, and hawks, and young horses sleeping in the field, but I wanted to see an oriole. When I get home, the tiny wildflowers in my pocket have almost disappeared.

C lear skies; they're hoping for rain.

I learned this by telephone from my hotel room. I forgot to bring my weather radio along, and I couldn't find, by phone, the barometer reading in the area. I did call a national rivers stages number to find out about the river levels, and listened to readings I didn't understand. Six point one, six point four, the Missouri eight point two, the Mississippi a fall of point three at Hannibal.

We left home at sunset Monday, driving south along the

bluffs of the Saint Croix River. The Mississippi comes in from the west at Hastings, Minnesota. It was a cool evening. There were baseball games from all over on the radio. A tankful of gas, a cooler full of cheese, crackers, orange juice. The dog comfortable on the back seat—he's going to Saint Louis! And his ears perk up when we say it.

We follow the Wisconsin side of the river, watching the last rose and purple of sunset, the gleam reflected in the west-facing windows of the white frame farmhouses built on the hillsides of this valley a century ago. The fading light leaves the moon in the sky—just the thinnest crescent, with Venus bright nearby.

We're traveling the Great River Road—that's the official designation. Had we time and endurance enough we could have taken our canoe out of the garage, carried it down to the water, and paddled to Saint Louis. Tied the boat up down by the Arch, and walked into town. Wouldn't that have been the way to see the river?

John Madson wrote a book a couple of years ago called *Up on the River: An Upper Mississippi Chronicle.* And what he really wanted to do was to take that same trip two hundred years ago. He writes:

> [It was] a rich, clean river moving easily to the sea, its first thousand miles broken occasionally by mild rapids where outcroppings of bedrock disputed its passage. River of giant sturgeon and catfish and paddlefish, of myriad bronze-backed bass and opal-eyed jack salmon with pearl mussels paving long reaches of its bed. Its sheer

cliffs held the eyries of peregrine falcons and
twisted cedars from which eagles watched the
limitless flights of wildfowl and passenger pi-
geons. The alluvial terraces of its tributaries
were winter quarters for the late woodland people who gathered in summer on the timbered
ridges above the River to memorialize honored
dead and celebrate brother creatures by building
great effigy mounds depicting falcons, snakes,
turtles and lines of marching bears . . . and not
far away those smiling sunlit prairie lands with
elk and bison and prairie chicken. . . . A region
of which the Mesquakies said: "The North is
too cold, the West too barren, the East too
bloody. This place is just right."

The river here is called the Upper Mississippi, down to
Cairo, where the Ohio comes in, that's south of Saint Louis.
Then, on to ninety miles south of New Orleans, it's the
Lower Mississippi. This was all explained to me the other
afternoon by a kindly towboat captain, Buddy Maynard,
working the river out in Saint Louis Harbor.

I wanted to ride along in the pilothouse of a towboat.
Captain Maynard was from Tennessee, *"Ten* nessee" as he
said it, married for thirty-seven years to "one little old Kentucky girl," third generation on the river, and his son is now
a pilot. Captain Maynard—bib overalls, a white shirt, lots
of pens and pencils, no hat, no pipe—explained some of his
work to me as we drank coffee and he *pushed* with his

towboat two barges downriver, fourteen hundred tons of coal each.

Captain Maynard has been on jobs up to the Twin Cities, eight days on the river at towboat speed. He said to me, "I'll tell you something. I don't think those Minnesota Twins are so hot."

We came down from the Twin Cities at a slow station-wagon speed. The Great River Road comes as close as it can to the water, some of it is even gravel. The road is a lot longer, a lot more fun that way.

One thing I don't like, though, so much about traveling. You get into these little motel rooms with mirrors in new places for you, and if you think you're maybe putting on weight, you'll know for sure when you surprise yourself in a full-length motel mirror. And this trip Will was shedding badly, losing his winter coat. We stopped once at a car wash to vacuum out the car, and when no one was looking, we vacuumed the dog. I think he liked it, made him feel important.

We drove 700 miles, coming into summer. And we passed the corn going north. We saw the first seedlings coming up in the fields at 470 miles. The corn got inches higher as we came into Missouri. The peonies were small green sprouts in Wisconsin, and in full fluffy white and pink and fuchsia blossom by Saint Louis.

The American West not that long ago was on the other side of the Mississippi. The western states were Illinois, Indiana, Ohio, Kentucky. But we also saw on this trip some moments of time's suspension. Glimpses from the car: a young mother sunbathing, lying on the grass on a quilt with a new baby; a father and son riding on a tractor together in the evening light; and a teenage couple sitting on a porch swing, I think holding hands.

Then a stop for coffee in an old Iowa river town. Quiet and proud neighbors. Older men riding bicycles. And about one-third of a high school band, the sophomores only, in jeans, shorts, tennis shoes, marching crookedly up the street, quite happily playing the theme of the Olympics.

On the second night we settled into a small farming town a few miles from the river, attracted there by the reputation of baked pork chops and celery seed dressing. It takes some walking after a meal like that, and we went out into the soft Iowa night. It's my favorite kind of town: the fields coming up to the back of the houses, cows just a few blocks off the Main Street. We walked along. The nighthawks were out, it was mostly dark. The air smelled freshly of peonies and manure. Our dog answered the gruff barks from backyards.

There's a commotion a few blocks away, lights flaring in the sky, people yelling, grass, dirt, wire fences, a scoreboard, bleachers—a softball game, fast pitch, full windup, uniforms, the whole works. A green and gold team plays against purple. There are first- and third-base coaches, two umpires, wives and mothers in the stands, and men who used to play, all drinking diet soda and light beer. Pizzas are delivered.

We sit close, first row, third-base side. We lean back on the bleachers, get to know the players in green: Jimmy Capp, the pitcher; Puck, the catcher; Bill at shortstop. Bill's a little heavy, but the game is played around him—he's in every play, it seems. In the seventh he's spiked by a runner and stays on the ground for a couple of minutes, his teammates gathered around. Bill gets up grinning, but tries to look stern.

The game moves on. We don't know the score, but we want the green team to win. We listen to the players: "Way to be . . . Way to hum . . . . Way to rear back, Jimmy Capp. . . . Way to hang." A small boy, wearing a green jersey, chases after foul balls. Children come up to the fence to tease their fathers on the bench. Twin girls in blue jeans and blue-jean jackets, three or four years old, long blonde Midwestern hair, are smiling and dancing.

The moon is above the trees over left field, a bright quarter moon now, with Venus still close. It will be the last play of the game. An infield fly—the softball white and spinning, high above the lights, players coming together near third, earnestly, the crowd yelling . . .

I used to watch a lot of softball games in the summer in the park near our house in the Ohio River town where I grew up. There is a difference for me now: when I was ten years old those men playing fast-pitch softball in the park were surely grownups—big, strong, fast, mature family men. More than thirty years later, men the same age now seem young—guys with wives and children but still playful and not at all serious. It's just—I guess—a matter of where you sit in the stands.

The water of the Saint Croix River is gray and still. And the toads are quiet this morning. At midnight I had to shut all the windows against the noise. I realized I was lying there in bed listening to *individual* toads with different pitches. These are called American toads. They've come down to the water to lay eggs. And sing. It's a high trilling sound, sort of like what you get if you blow lightly into a referee's whistle.

Each trill goes on about twenty seconds, but the toads

have a super choir director and the trilling overlaps. The sound is constant. The dog is grumpily shifting around on the floor of the bedroom, doing a lot of sighing and scratching. I think Will must be hearing the *complete* audio spectrum of the trilling.

The toads started about ten o'clock on the night of the full moon, which is always a strange time anyway. Just after the moon came cruising over the ridge to the east, we turned down the baseball game to listen. The toads were loud and resonant. Their sound took over the night. And after an hour or so, as we sat in the dark listening, it seemed the trilling became demanding, as if the sound were calling something forth.

I had been thinking about trolls anyway, trolls that live in literature—and under bridges when you're growing up. Driving back from Saint Louis a couple of weeks ago, we stopped for the night in Iowa City, and that evening went to see the movie *Willow*. There are trolls in that film. Indeed, we see the first one under a bridge. Our hero on the screen can't see it until it's almost too late. It's just about as awful, this troll of George Lucas' imagination, as the ones we saw in our minds. No, it's more awful, slimy, hairy, red-eyed, a creature of true loathing.

I thought about the trolls when I went outside the house to see if I could find some of the toads, but they heard or saw me coming and the trilling stopped, or moved away. You could hear the toads plopping into the water. They hide when a predator is nearby.

To a toad, I must be as frightening as a troll. And how must grownup people seem to a wood tick? The wood ticks, this time of year, courageously wait in the tall grass to leap upon passersby, dogs or people. They climb on, all eight legs scrambling. They find a quiet dark place on your body, take a satisfying bite, and settle down until satiated with blood.

You don't feel the bite. It could be dangerous. Best to have a partner during tick season. She checks me, I check her. We both inspect the dog, who wants to check the cat.

There is an intensity of life early in June, the toads mating, the ticks leaping, lilies bursting open in the woods, the silky seed pods of the cottonwood floating in the air.

And all of this happens without water, almost. We've had a month without rain. I watch the water towers of the towns out in the valley, wondering. And it is early one afternoon, with rain threatening, that I get into a bright orange pickup truck and ride out to a water tower, one of three in a town of twelve thousand people.

The fellow in charge of the utilities department is going to take a look around his tower, and I can go along. The tower is on a hill at the edge of town, with fences and locked gates, important mostly once a year at high school graduation time. It's a big tower, 750,000 gallons. The water comes not from the river but from wells, several of them, reaching down into the Jordan Sandstone Aquifer. The water's clean, doesn't need to be treated, except for fluoridation.

Down in the aquifer the water level is not affected by the drought. But city officials worry about sprinkling. A town sprinkling its lawns can use four or five times as much water as normal, and it could be more than the system can pump and store.

We look around inside the base of the tower. There's a

metal skirt extending down from the tank itself, so we're in a big white room with a dirt floor. The bottom of the tank is high above. Actually, there's a blue nylon rain fly above, to collect condensation from the tank.

"Want to go on up?" he asks.

"Sure." The ladder's at the side. "You go first, I'll be along," I say.

Straight up. One story, then two, three, four; step off to rest. One more, then a platform, and a bridge out over to the bottom of the tank. We go on. The ladder now reaches straight up inside a round hole in the middle of the water tank. It's hard to get the rhythm of the climbing. It's a bit slippery; you want to make sure you're holding on to something at the same time you step up. We stop to rest, and to do a lot of breathing.

"You doing okay?" he pants.

"Yeah."

He tells me he's a little out of shape now, but in the fall, to get ready for elk hunting in the mountains in Montana, he comes out and climbs these ladders several times a day.

We go on up, and clamber out through a port at the top, careful in the wind. We're 180 feet high. It's overcast, but we can see the tall buildings of Minneapolis, twenty-two miles away. It's all river and farmland around, the wind rippling the alfalfa. I'm not sure I'd want to be up here at night, a high school senior with a can of spray paint.

I had hopes of this being a romantic experience. The water tower is symbolic of community, of teenage adventure, of a first kiss. But mostly I'm still trying to figure out the physics of the thing.

I was shown one large pipe down below. One pipe fills the tower, the same pipe empties the tower. The water flows one way or the other, on demand. The engineer sketches a diagram for me, but he can see confusion in my eyes as I nod my head. We climb down slowly, my legs shaking, and say goodbye.

The rain has started, splashing on dusty windshields. It gets heavier as I drive through town, the water running down the gutters, the water that years ago my grandmother in a neighborhood like this one would warn us not to play in. We liked to make little boats of paper and float them downstream into the drains.

I recall a line from a Harry Nilsson song called "Think About Your Troubles":

> *You can take your teardrops*
> *And drop 'em in a teacup*
> *Take 'em down—to the riverside*
> *And throw 'em over the side*
> *To be swept up by a current*
> *To be eaten by some fishes.*

The afternoon air is now steamy, full of dust and pollen and moisture. The toads will be happy. And by way of congratulation, for the rain and the climb up the tower, having guessed at how many calories I used, even though I've had lunch, I go off in search of a chili dog and an ice cream cone.

A quiet morning, a hot dry day coming.

The river will be busy, the water will lose its early composure to fast, snarling boats with skiers behind. The sailboats stay out of the way, the canoes stay on shore. I think I'll stay on the porch, screened and shaded with a stone floor still cold from spring. I could sit here, drink iced coffee, read for a couple of hours. I have some newly acquired field guides— the Audubon series—North American trees, wildflowers, butterflies.

The first thing I can learn about butterflies will be progress. I don't know any by sight. And they seem just like magic in the sunlight. If you could put a bird and a flower together, you'd have a butterfly. And they have great names: the blue-dusted roadside skipper, blueberry sulphur, West Virginia white, northern checkerspot, nokomis fritillary, American painted lady.

I bought the field guides out of frustration. I've been reading a new biography of Aldo Leopold, the writer, scientist, conservationist. Very early as he was growing up, along the Mississippi, he knew the trees, the birds and flowers. He was a naturalist the way another child is a musician. And when I look at the woods, I see only trees: I want to be seeing poplars and hawthorns, sandbar willow and catalpa.

We've been cautiously adventurous lately, exploring cool dark garages in town. The door's open, sale tables are set out, kids are selling lemonade. You have to stay in control at a garage sale. Don't bother with those racks of clothes out front. You don't want that eight-track tape player, you don't need the table saw—you'd just get in trouble.

But back there, at five minutes past the start of the sale on the morning of the first day, a waffle iron! This can be exciting if you've been looking for about two years for a waffle iron that does not have nonstick coating. Even if you've bought two or three before and they haven't worked at all, and the last one you threw disgustedly in the trash because it was a complete pasty, goopy mess.

You still have hope, and this one is two dollars. Nice condition. Wooden handles. Complete with cord. The next morning, while Neenah's still asleep, I mix up some batter.

Put in lots of butter so it won't stick, and turn on the waffle iron. Let it warm up, pour the batter in. Put down the top, wait five minutes. The steam stops. No smoke yet. Lift the lid. And there's a perfect toasty, golden waffle.

I go wake her up. "Want some waffles for breakfast? Oh, yeah, it works, I was sure it would."

So we have the waffle iron, and now I need to find a red and white checked tablecloth and some white curtains. And I'd like to have one of those old kitchen clocks that you plug in and the second hand makes a little buzzing sound going around.

All this to go with a garden just outside the kitchen window. A garden that looks fine so far, but we put it in quickly on Memorial Day, and I thought I should go and have the soil tested over at the university.

They were having a quiet day at the lab, and the technicians had time to talk. They do twenty thousand soil tests a year. Twenty thousand little bags of dirt arrive in the mail, mostly in the fall and spring. We walk my sample through the testing process, it becomes number 16200. It is crushed, and strained, and filtered, and precipitated. The pH is determined. My stomach, they say, has a pH of 2. My garden soil is 6.7. Rainfall is 5.7, unless it's acid rain that's falling. As far as pH is concerned, blueberries and alfalfa would not be caught in the same field together.

We use a spectrophotometer to measure wave length and intensity of light, and thus amounts of potassium and phosphorus. A young technician, his right hand wet and dirty most of the year, judges by feel that my garden is sandy loam, and he grades it "medium" in organic matter. He has a drawerful of samples to use in comparison, all the Minnesota soil colors including red from the iron range in the north.

The computer prints out the rest. Potassium, for example, is in the soil at 350 pounds per acre, or would be if I had an acre. It's a pretty good garden for sweet corn and tomatoes. The laboratory computer is recommending a mid-season application of nitrogen, to be watered into the soil. But it looks good. If you're buying spaghetti sauce futures from our garden, you'll do fine.

Soil testing can get to be pretty complex. If you wanted to—and many people do because of the toxic waste problem—you could discover intensities of all sorts of things. Lithium in the soil, titanium, boron. Silicon, of course (that's sand), but also arsenic and beryllium and strontium, chromium, lead, copper, zinc. The *amounts* of the elements are crucial. Just enough—a nutrient; too much—a poison. And, in the end, it is just soil. How does it make a marigold happy, a cucumber prosper, oregano thrive, and ripe tomatoes come tumbling off the vine? My scientist friend at the lab said in the old days, if you were lucky, a buffalo would die on your land. It's just a matter of the concentration of nutrients.

Lacking a dead buffalo, late this morning I went over to the composting site in Saint Paul. People bring their grass clippings and leaves here, and people take away compost, in different degrees of decay. I want some grass clippings and some rich leaf mulch. There's a small baby bird nestled in the moist warm leaves, scared. I take it over to the grass by the fence.

One night we go for a walk out on the road along the

ridge. The dog comes with us, happy that it's cooler. The wind is up high, rustling in the cottonwoods. The field guides say that cottonwood leaves have a characteristic rustling sound. I always think of cattle rustling, because in the westerns I read years ago, the cowboys would camp at night, down by the creek bed under the cottonwood trees.

The river below us is silver, and so much light remains in the sky at seventeen minutes until ten o'clock that we have shadows, walking down the road. It's quiet, just the whisper in the trees and crickets far away. It's easy now to imagine the Saint Croix River Valley as it once was. There's a phrase in Aldo Leopold's *Sand County Almanac* about virgin country, "where nameless men by nameless rivers wander / and in strange valleys die strange deaths—alone."

We will all be gone someday, and we can only hope that to the earth, it does not matter that we've been here.

The sun rises today at 5:26 A.M. Summer begins Monday evening. The days will shorten by two minutes for a week or so, then by three.

The solstice confuses me sometimes. Why does summer start when the days get shorter? If summer's here, why is the hottest weather still a month away? But then winter's like that too, starting in the dark with the coldest days coming later.

If you're outside in the evening, the light stays longer.

Remember when you were a child and your mother would call for you to come in, saying it was dark already, and it was—if you were inside the house looking out.

We've been just watching the Saint Croix River in the late afternoons this week: the sailboats, the hot-air balloons, the ducks on the water. We took a couple of old lawn chairs down to the sand, to leave there. We found the chairs for fifty cents apiece somewhere; someone was glad to see them go.

I was trying the other day to get rid of some old *National Geographic* magazines. They take up a lot of space, and they're too heavy to ever move. So I bundled up about fifty of them to throw out.

The secret here is not to look at the list of contents on the binding or you'll never be able to. See, look, "Mount Saint Michel," "Bluebirds," June 1977, better keep this one. And March 1983, "Ghost Ships," "Sled Race," this is research, have to hang on to this one. You can imagine the guys who come along to pick up the trash having the same problem. "Look, Fred, here's 'Milwaukee' and 'Meteorites'!" So you don't have to be guilty about throwing out the old *Geographics*. They don't really ever go anywhere.

There's a summer story that I've remembered, thinking about the evenings and the light. It's Ray Bradbury's fantasy "Something Wicked This Way Comes." The story involves two small boys, Will and Jim, and a lightning rod salesman and a carnival coming to town on a train. Bradbury writes:

> Midnight then and the town clocks chiming on
> toward one and two and then three in the deep

morning and the peals of the great clocks shaking dust off old toys in high attics and shedding silver off old mirrors in yet higher attics and stirring up dreams about clocks in all the beds where children slept.

Will heard it.

Muffled away in the prairie lands, the chuffing of an engine, the slow-following dragonglide of a train.

Will sat up in bed.

Across the way, like a mirror image, Jim sat up too.

A calliope began to play oh so softly, grieving to itself, a million miles away.

Walk around in a small town in the early evening, past lovely old white lawn furniture, a green and white glider on a porch. You'll find neighborhoods from the 1950s. Some garages with peeling paint, a trellis waiting for morning glories. The last of the peonies favoring front-yard flower beds, harmonizing with the creamy blossoms of the catalpa trees. Kids with no shirts and burr haircuts and babies with underpants will be running in and out of the sprinkler. And a hand-painted sign will offer "Puppies for Sale," brown and black and white springer spaniels, with a happy mother.

In the memories of my childhood, of a small town in June, the lights are up, red, green, yellow, strung from trees and poles around the yard and up the driveway of the old red brick house on the corner by the park. It's Friday night—an ice cream social. My grandmother's church circle

looked after and raised money for the "Old Ladies' Home."
That's what it was called then.

The funeral home would bring over some chairs and
folding tables. Some large cardboard tubs of ice cream would
be delivered. Chocolate, vanilla, and neapolitan, which was,
am I right about this, chocolate, vanilla, and strawberry?
The women of the circle would bring tablecloths from
home, and their cakes: angel food, cakes with coconut
frosted icing, devil's food cake with white icing.

Ice cream, cake, a Coca-Cola or coffee, all for twenty-five
cents a ticket. Couples would come from the neighborhood
or from the church, and families would stop by after the
softball games. My twin brother and I would go along to
help my grandmother. We'd set up chairs and put out the
plates and napkins. We were eight years old, nine maybe,
not dressed alike but surely twins, with blond hair and blue
eyes, and we were paid a great deal of attention by the
women of the church circle and by the older ladies of the
home. We'd smile, waiting for leftover cake and ice cream.

Many of these women, the younger ones, I would see
years later, when it became their time, along with my grandmother, to sell their houses and go and live in the home.
Friends, together now. I'd visit, and they'd say, "Oh, now
which one are you?" And they'd remember, well and strong-
ly, those Friday nights in June thirty years before.

My grandfather had a friend, a bachelor. No one in the
town knew much about him; they said he had some money.
He and my grandfather would spend time together. He
knew of my grandmother's interest in the Old Ladies'
Home. And when he died, not having a family, he left the

home a considerable amount of money, with a stipulation—
that elderly men be taken in as well. And it was done. The
money helped with a new building. And the new sign read,
"King's Daughters' Home for the Aged."

My grandmother left the home several years ago. She
outlived her friends, didn't know the younger folks coming
in. She now spends half the year with her son, the other time
with her daughter. I hope to see her very soon, and have
some ice cream.

I t's a soft and fresh morning. These days, early, before seven, it always seems as though it *could* rain.

It was a restless night. Fireworks were booming out in the valley, even though it was a couple of nights early. Will especially didn't like the noise; he'd bark at each new threat.

Dogs can hear what we don't, and they pay closer attention. Ever notice a dog's ears when you just touch a paper bag or a plastic wrapper?

We're planning our own fireworks display for Will. I

think he'll enjoy watching those snakes. You know, those black curly things. I lit one the other night for practice, and as it burned I was amazed at my memory of the smell waiting there in my mind.

Here's another one, just two words I ran across this week in a book: "construction paper." Think of it, and the years are gone. You remember the colors, even how it tasted.

You could be in the weather business in the upper Midwest these days of June and May without even owning a rain gauge. It didn't rain enough to even dampen a sheet of newspaper left out on the lawn. The grass is the color of late winter, and it crunches the same way too when you walk on it. Some rain clouds have gone over, heading east. The cornfields, the soybeans, gasp as the moisture moves on.

Wednesday morning, though, in the dark kitchen, making coffee, I heard some good news on the radio. It's good, waking up to find out that the Twins won the late game on the coast and that it's been raining over much of Minnesota, out to the west. There was also a report of frost, way up north in the state.

The rain had moved along the valley of the Minnesota River, south and west of the Twin Cities. I kept the radio on that morning and drove down through the valley, listening to the farm reports, seeing the puddles along the side of the road. I stopped for lunch, for the special—roast pork and dressing and mashed potatoes and gravy and iced tea.

I've been clipping instructions for making perfect iced tea. And I found a recipe for making fresh pea soup chilled, with celery. There is nothing more peaceful in the summer in the evenings than sitting out by the garden shelling sweet peas for supper, your hands finding an old rhythm.

In the restaurant, at the counter, all around, there is talk of rain.

"How much did you get down your way?"

"Only four-tenths, really? I think we got almost two inches."

"I heard three up north of Mankato." There's no talk of baseball. These men are now expecting the Twins to win, they are not expecting rain.

Fifteen more miles and the Minnesota River Valley deepens down to the town of LeSueur, the home of canned peas, the home of the Jolly Green Giant. He stands tall on a billboard by the highway, but the surrounding fields are in beans.

Thirty more miles south, away from the valley now, I come around a turn and see across the farmland, about four miles away, a face! A man's face, dark, wearing a hat. I'm looking at the grain elevator in the town of Good Thunder, Minnesota. Good Thunder, population 650, in Blue Earth County.

There is a mural, almost completed, on the buildings and silos of the Good Thunder Feed and Grain Company. Paintings of Indians and old farmers, pigs and draft horses, the hotel and a veteran's brass band, and blue sky and corn and grandparents and kids and a computer. I walk around to see it, then back up to get some distance.

There's a moving figure in one scene. And I realize it's the artist, he's still painting. Ta-coumba Aiken is standing in a small cage, a bucket, suspended by a hydraulic crane on the ground. He controls it from up there. We talk a bit, yelling. He's two stories up.

Good Thunder, he says, was a Dakota Indian who tried hard to keep the peace with the settlers in the 1860s. Good Thunder took part in a celebration of friendship, a parade through town. The artist tells me this with enthusiasm, as if for the first time, but I figure he's got to be tired of people wandering by shouting up questions.

So I say, "When do you hope to finish?"

"Five o'clock."

"No—the whole project?"

"Five o'clock—this is supposed to be the last day. My wife wants me home."

Good luck, I say, although I feel like grabbing a brush and helping out with that large patch of green up there by him.

In the car driving home I'm trying to figure out how, exactly, to teach Will to carry a small flag in his mouth in the parade on the Fourth. He'd have to learn quick. I saw it done once in Virginia, a happy black Lab prancing along with an American flag. The parade we're going to would be perfect. It's in a small Minnesota town where everyone marches down the street, and then the parade turns around and comes back. You see everything twice. One highlight every year is the school nurse, walking by herself, waving, wearing her white uniform and carrying a parasol.

Also on the drive home the book *Dune* comes to mind, the science fiction story by Frank Herbert, written twenty years ago. It's about the planet Dune, far in the future. Once it was a world with water, but now it's a desert, with giant sandworms and temperatures of 350 degrees, and you live in a suit that distills the moisture from your body so you can drink it. Life on Dune is a struggle for water, food, safety, and freedom.

It would be nice, wouldn't it—a cooling, drenching rain, enough water so you wouldn't have to worry about the tomatoes for a week. Enough so that you could go to sleep listening . . . to water falling.

9 July—Winnipeg

16 degrees Celsius

The barometer reading 30.05 and rising

W̲e are in a room in a hotel near the airport, outside the city of Winnipeg, in the province of Manitoba in Canada. Finally there is fresh cool air in the mornings, almost chilly at night. You can stand on the prairie and watch the weather someone else is having, many miles away. The Winnipeg Folk Festival is known for rain, and that was a delightful anticipation one morning this week, driving north, recalling last summer when we first came to Winnipeg, to watch, to listen to the music, to sit in a quiet rain with thousands of people.

At home this week, it was an awfully hot and crackling dry Fourth of July, ending with fireworks exploding high over the Saint Croix River. The next day the town began to settle down into July and the rest of the summer, without apparent enthusiasm. A small carnival, after a week's run, was being slowly loaded up to move on.

There was a reassuring moment as we left town. The first sweet corn was for sale. Good-looking corn, but the ears were small. A dollar a half dozen. And for the first of the season. What would you pay? The young farmer had driven up from Pepin, Wisconsin. He said the corn was only about three feet high or so, but it was ready to pick. About the rain, he said that down his way, "we've been having two-tenths of an inch every month, whether we need it or not."

So we're off with corn and some fresh peas and lots of water in the cooler. The dog is at home being looked after by a friend. It would have been too hot. Will came with us last summer, and Winnipeg to him means sitting in the car. A folk festival is the same as cross-country skiing, just hours and hours of waiting for us.

I like the idea of getting in the car and driving some place to hear music. I used to go to a lot of bluegrass festivals and spend the weekend. A bluegrass bass player I knew said once when they'd played festivals all summer, the music was around so much you'd hear the songs in the wind coming in through the windows of the van.

We drove a good ways, fast, before lunch, listening to

rock music and the weather reports. One local announcer, a very young deejay, as he was signing off, said his motto was "Remember, it's better to burn out than fade away." And the women who give the stock market updates and commodity reports on the radio, talking with confidence about July soybeans and Minneapolis wheat, seem to be getting younger.

We found a town with a park by the lake for our picnic. There was a mean dry and hot wind blowing. The water was low, green with algae. A strip of sand, some grass, a parking lot, and about one hundred teenagers who were concerned, it seemed, with a great deal of intensity, about the way they looked.

I had never before seen teenage boys walk down to the beach in sunglasses, bright shorts, gold chains, to put on lotion and then lie down on towels in the sun. Several groups of boys, not reading, not talking, just doing what only girls used to call "laying out." They did have great tans—already a summer's worth.

I am someone frightened by the sun, now. But I do sort of like the way my left arm looks after I've been driving for a day or so, especially traveling west and north. But the sun is too hot through the window at three o'clock. There's a town ahead, I remember, where the elm trees still thrive. There's cool shade on the streets. We find a café and a bakery. We eat peanut butter cookies and drink coffee—hot coffee; strangely, it seems to help. Everyone talks about the weather. Yesterday a hundred and six, they said. And the baker said his air-conditioning was working at four in the morning but not much after.

Back in the car, as we turn north along the Red River, we pass through a rainstorm moving east. There is not much rain, but some farmers are happy for five minutes. Those of us on the highway watch the splatters on the windshield, the big raindrops coming down like wet June bugs.

The Red River flows north into Canada through Winnipeg. I always wonder, in summers when it doesn't rain, how the water keeps on flowing in the rivers. Where does it come from? But that's less of a mystery here; the Red River is quite dry, almost dazed in its bed. This is the river that Eric Sevareid, the CBS newsman, wrote about. Back when he was eighteen, in the summer and fall of 1930, he traveled with a friend up the Red River to Winnipeg, and beyond to Hudson Bay. The book is called *Canoeing with the Cree.* Their trip was a hot one too, but also cold, at times desperately so.

For us the weather cools after two or three hours. We're getting close to Canada, driving through the small towns named for places in Scotland or France, towns that are proud of their nine-man football teams.

It may be the light, but the grass does seem somewhat green now. We stop alongside a creek. There's water here, high in the banks, and it's cool. The swallows are out, and mourning doves. In the west dark clouds to the top of the sky are backlit by sunset. There is thunder behind us, to the south. And for the first time in a long while there is the sweet smell of grass.

The next day we went to visit a village east of Winnipeg, a reconstructed pioneer settlement dating from 1873, settled by Mennonites from south Russia. A marvelous windmill has been restored. Its blades, the wings of the windmill, are sixty feet long. The millstone, for grinding wheat into flour, weighs about two tons. It is wonderfully accessible technology. The great wooden gears turn, lubricated only by beeswax.

The windmills of Eastern Europe, and possibly here, were also used to send messages. If the wings were slightly less than vertical or horizontal, to the clockwise side, that meant a baby had been born in the village.

I've always wanted, in a place of history like this, to go back in time for just an instant, to be there on a muddy street in the summer of 1888, hearing Dutch and German, watching the first windmill turn. But also, when you go down into the sod house, half of it underground and damp and surely cold, you think of what it could have been like to be in a strange country, on the prairie: alone, without books, without music, with the wind.

A singer on the stage of the Winnipeg Folk Festival looks out to the west and north, watching the weather, the gray clouds and rainbows. In the longer view, there is the expanse of territory settled by the Inuit long ago, and then the Scottish colonists and the English, the French, the homesteaders from Germany and Russia, from Poland. The music recalls the land. The people and the music come together like the rivers, gathering at Winnipeg.

16 July

74 degrees

The barometer reading 29.90 and rising

The night was desperately hot.

Yesterday a dry and discouraging wind was blowing. It was 102 degrees. The alarm of the weather radio in the kitchen went off. There were thunderstorms coming, "Thunderstorms firing on the edge of the front," as they say, ". . . violent at times. Plan to take interior cover."

But most of the weather was thirty miles to the west, and we didn't even have rain, after the alert people were outside their houses watching the strange clouds moving across the valley. Puffy clouds, gray and yellow with light shining through like lovely dangerous marshmallows in the sky.

I've been reading this week about space missions, to Mars and beyond, and can easily imagine the weather on earth to be organic. As if the weather were a creature of infinite size, mischievous, angry, and bored.

I drop an ice cube on the floor for the dog, and listen to the grateful crunching. He likes ice cubes, but usually he won't finish one. He just leaves it, melting. We now have an air-conditioned room, and the door stays shut until bedtime, when it is Will's delight to go in and, with great sighs, settle down in a curl in the corner on the floor. Dogs get tired easily, and grumpy, in the hot weather.

We are all probably spoiled, though. I'll be in the kitchen in the morning feeling hot but soon to be in a nice cool office, and on the radio I'll hear the announcements for the corn-detasseling crews to meet. Crew numbers, locations, times. How would it be at the end of such a day, riding home in the back of a pickup truck after hours in the dusty cornrows?

Our garden is going well. The weather makes you pay attention, watering by hand, slow, trickling, soaking the tomatoes and green peppers, snapdragons and marigolds. We've made pesto already, with basil, olive oil, pine nuts, and grated cheese.

With basil, if you get out in front of the bitterness— harvest it early—you'll have the essence of summer. The taste itself is green and growing. We'll have pesto tomorrow for Sunday dinner, with chicken and corn from the market, and maybe I'll fry up some green tomatoes.

I went to visit some honey bees this week with a friend, Jim Fitzpatrick, who takes care of the hives at the nature center. Every ten days or so he goes out to visit with the bees, and to check on the honey. I go along with him because I've never seen a beehive up close, and we both have been wondering about the effects of the hot, dry summer on the inhabitants.

Our equipment: gloves, a hat and veil, and a bee suit made from white canvas. We take a smoker and some wood chips for fuel, some bee medicine, some extra honey racks, called "supers," and go on out in the field to the hives. It's a day of sunshine, and that's good because Jim says on cloudy days the bees all stay home inside. They use the sun for navigation. There are four hives, side by side. Stacks of white-painted wooden boxes. Perhaps four hundred thousand honey bees are somewhere right close around.

Jim takes the top off one hive to look inside. These are boxes full of racks. The racks look sort of like sliding window screens, and the bees build their honeycombs on these wooden frames. These are Italian bees, and their honeycomb cells are about 5.2 millimeters in diameter. The cells are hexagonal, the most efficient use of space.

Jim puffs some smoke down inside. This will confuse the bees somewhat, but they're quite busy anyway, depositing nectar in the cells, packing pollen away. Some bees are tending the queen, some are guarding the hive, some are cleaning up. Some are even undertakers, taking dead bees outside and dropping them in burial.

Some are scout bees, in search of flowers and nectar.

When the scouts come back to report success, they do a little dance for the other bees, a dance that describes the flowers they've found, and the location.

A lot of bees are on ventilation duty, fanning with their wings to cool the hive and help evaporate moisture from the honey.

There is not as much honey in the frames as Jim might find in a summer of normal rainfall. Not as many flowers, not as much nectar. But the bees look good and healthy.

An hour goes by. Jim is inspecting all the hive boxes. It's a hot job and the sweat drips, and you can't scratch your nose because of the hat and veil. Only a few bees are flying around.

Jim has told me you don't build up a tolerance to bee stings. It works the other way. He talks of someone found— in time—unconscious on the kitchen floor. She was a bee-keeper stung only once that day. The next one could be fatal.

We are now up to our noses in bees, pulling out the frames, looking for the queen, and it gets steamy and musky and more and more bees are in the air, striking at our veils and stinging the gloves. I try to stand very still, and breathe slowly.

Jim drops one of the frames just a bit, and the bees don't like it. Their noise—the wings buzzing, the vibration of their bodies—is both natural and unworldly. I lean down to the hive to hear the sound. The frequencies change, become deeper. The sound has mystery. It is a sound you could hear in one of the *Star Wars* movies. Maybe you did, the ship moving through the star field, and the sound of deep space, all around?

We don't find the queen in any of the hives. She must be busy laying eggs. We do find some extra queen cells that the worker bees, always plotting, are getting ready in case more queens are deemed necessary. This is the original palace intrigue, inside a beehive. If you watch carefully, you can see some bees being born, little ones chewing their way up out of their cells. They stumble around a bit, and then go off looking for work. Their first day of life is their first day on the job.

Jim puts the hives back together and sprinkles on each one a mixture of powdered sugar and Terramycin, against bacterial infection. Some bees become covered by the powder and fly around—ghost bees—dusty white and dazed. We leave and take off the bee suits, bring the equipment back along with a few racks of honey.

Most of the bees will die by early winter, in the cold weather. The twenty thousand or so left in each hive will stay in a swarm around the queen, feeding her, keeping her warm. Perhaps our visit today, to a honey bee, is like a dangerous thunderstorm passing over. After we're gone the signal bees pass the word: It's all clear, the storm's over, you can return safely to your homes.

23 July

61 degrees

The barometer reading 30.07 and rising

I t's soft and damp, a morning to walk out in the yard with bare feet and wander around to see how things are doing after the rain.

You just know that water from the sky is better for everything than water from the hose. And did your mother ever, when you were young, wash and then rinse your hair with a panful of rainwater?

The new lilac bush over by the fence seems fine. The lilies and tuberous begonia—red, white, yellow—are all okay.

The tomatoes are still green but getting big fast. Leeks, dill, chamomile, parsley, marjoram, all thrive. The pumpkin is promising. The earth in the garden is black and healthy. The grass of the yard is turning up green again; it's been dormant.

It rained Wednesday in the afternoon, and then once at night, with thunder rolling by over a valley where a thousand air conditioners made a rumbling sound in the dark. And there was rain on the river, and last evening almost a celebration. There were sailboats and water skiers out on the Saint Croix, hot-air balloons high above the water, and flying lower than the balloons some ultralight aircraft, at least one of them equipped with pontoons. Then at sunset two old biplanes crossed the valley at about a thousand feet—a red plane and a blue one—flying west with the light.

Thursday morning I drive north and west. There is still some water on the road. The farm stands are open, offering "sweet corn," a proud fact. The towns get smaller as I drive. Lots of old trucks are for sale. A big doghouse out in back of one place has "Luther" painted over the door; painted, it looks like, by Luther himself. I follow my map, looking for county road numbers now, and find the sign that says, "Prairie Restorations, Incorporated."

Someone told me once, "You ought to see the prairie a day or so after a rain." And the prairie survives here in patches, remnants they call them. It survives too in cultivated fifty-acre plots, and in forty-pound bags of seed, ready to ship out. In all the prairie states, there are protected preserves of grass, many around Minnesota. But this is a company that helps preserve the prairies by making more.

If you're building a corporate headquarters in, say, North

Dakota, and you don't have trees and don't want to water grass and mow it, you call up this company and they'll come. Starting with bare ground, they'll put in seeds and grasses and flowers. The North Dakota site? Forty thousand seedlings put in by hand.

The fellow who has been at this for about twenty years is Ron Bowen. He's having some coffee and a sweet roll, happy to be outside on a cool sunny day, wearing shorts and a Will Steger "North Pole '86" red T-shirt. His shoes are in the back of his pickup. They've had three inches of rain here in three weeks, and there are lots of wildflowers showing, mixed in with the grasses. But it's only temporary color in a dry season. A tough year, he says, a wonderful learning time.

We walk around his fields, grasshoppers flying up to make a feast for the bluebirds. There are acres of big bluestem growing. It's the basic tallgrass of the prairie. Thousands of pounds of seed will be harvested here. A few acres of blazing star, a purple prairie flower, growing for seed. Other varieties are dotted about in small plots.

The plant list—hundreds of names—will take your mind away for a while, your thoughts moving with the wind across the grass: prairie sage, swamp milkweed, marsh marigold, larkspur, butterfly weed, wild strawberry, Canadian rye, golden Alexander, black-eyed Susan, mountain mint, columbine, frostweed, sweet everlasting, wild lupine, Indian grass, prairie smoke. The Latin names are listed as well. All of these are native plants, which is to say they were here before European settlement, in the 1850s.

In the few places left where the prairie is wild, seventeen

new flowers a week come into bloom between March and October. The word "prairie" itself is French for meadow. And the grasses alone are worth a summer's study—the different greens of the grass. As Paul Gruchow points out in his book *Journal of a Prairie Year:* "There is nothing so impoverished of distinction as simply the color green. There are greens as there are grains of sand. . . . Even one green is not the same green. There is the green of young life, of maturity, of old age. There is the green of new rain and of long drought. . . . There is a language in it, a poetry, a music. We have not stopped long enough to hear it."

Ron Bowen and I sit and talk of prairie sites to visit in this state, and down in Iowa and South Dakota. He knows them all, he goes to them like church.

After a couple of hours of asphalt-hot driving, the day comes to an end over in Wisconsin. We go to the first county fair we've found in either state. It is in a valley that honors farming—this is where you could make a good movie about it, the small communities and country stores, the white frame farmhouses, golden bales of hay in the fields, mist rising off the creeks as it gets dark.

There was a note in the paper this week, "U.S. farm population slides to lowest post–Civil War level." Only 2 percent of us are farming now. In 1820 that figure was 72 percent; in 1920, 30 percent.

At the fairgrounds we wander through the midway, lose a dollar to a softball throw, have some coconut cream pie and some apple pie and coffee at the First Lutheran Church dining hall. We talk to Billie the donkey at the petting zoo, walk into the livestock barns to see the young kids taking care of their cows, go through the senior craft building and the homemakers' exhibits.

And we walk out behind the tractor exhibit, there are some low bleachers and a stage. Some very earnest teenagers are up there dancing and singing. Fourteen or fifteen years old, about twenty of them, wearing black pants, white formal shirts, bright blue sashes. There's a piano, drums, guitar. They play show tunes, folk songs, some rock and roll. All the songs are short. Some of the voices wander a bit off pitch. It's a singing group of 4-H youngsters, sponsored by an insurance company. They're traveling around to different fairs.

You start to walk away. But they're smiling so seriously, and you sit down on the grass. The last light of the day is over the hill. A half moon rises in the sky. You can hear the crickets, even with all the county fair sounds, and the entertainers dance up to the microphones and sing:

> *River in the rain*
> *Sometimes at night you look like a long white*
>   *train,*
> *Winding your way,*
> *Away*
> *Somewhere.*
> *River I love you, don't you care?*

One morning under seventy does not cool the memory. There have been thirty-one days of temperatures above ninety degrees this summer. The cool air in our air-conditioned room is like a creature trying to escape from under the door.

Summer's high point is past by just a few days. In the north of Minnesota the blueberries, growing wild, being harvested with blueberry scoops by people and with claws by bears, are said to be plentiful, in time for a festival in the town of Ely.

I tried to get some of those blueberries, but they could have been truffles in France. No one in the Twin Cities sold the berries that grow just two hundred miles to the north. And so we had some from Oregon with ice cream last night, big and plump and not the same. The chilled fresh pea soup that I made turned out okay, though: peas, carrots, onions, potatoes, chicken stock, sour cream. It was cool and pale green, with chives on top.

You can come back from the garden now with your hands smelling pretty good from the chives, Greek oregano, basil, and tomatoes. The energy of this week in summer is impressive. Even badly hurt by drought, the upper Midwest seems wonderfully alive, in blossom and bearing fruit. It's almost as if you could go out to a field near the woods, lie down in the grass, be still, and you would grow.

But that's deceptive. It's dry. And it could be the trees that will suffer the most. You should water the young ones. They'll have a good chance. But for many of the older trees in the town, the drought could be the last difficulty. Elm trees, diseased, clearly dying, are marked now by a circle of orange paint. These trees are coming down, and I watched three of them fall yesterday morning. Men with chain saws and a high-reaching truck. Quick, neat work, big sections crashing to the ground. From a tree to firewood in seconds.

The foreman, who stayed below, was wary of questions about the age of the elm trees. He's probably had lots of folks come up to his crew wanting to stop even dead trees from being taken down. There's a small poem by Michael

Dennis Browne that perhaps was written after watching some trees fall. It's called *Child's Elm Song:*

> *If there were no trees*
> *I would take my turn*
> *And stand in the street in spring*
> *With arms wide open*
> *In case there were birds*
> *Who needed a place to sing.*

I think this little town would try hard to keep its elm trees. Clothes drying outside on the line is still something that makes sense to people here. And I was thinking about that this week, reading in the paper about a place in the East that was going to make playing basketball outdoors against the law.

I spent a lot of time, growing up, playing basketball on the court behind our house. Playing well into darkness, and in cold and rain. I continued to dream and play, even though I stopped growing at a noncompetitive height. And now, often, when I see kids playing ball in someone's driveway or a park, I remember something that happened in Washington, D.C., about ten years ago. A man was killed by someone who was robbing his house. It was a stupid, tragic death. He was a doctor, young, a writer, well liked. And as tribute was paid, this story was told.

He loved basketball, loved kids. He would go to the sporting goods store and buy basketball nets, the real cotton cord nets. He'd put them in the back of his station wagon along with a stepladder, and at night he would drive around the city, stopping at playgrounds and parks, to find a basket-ball goal that was just a bare rim. He'd set up his ladder and put up a net. He believed that youngsters should know the feeling, the sound, the ripping swish, of a basketball going through a net.

Another poem has come to mind this week. It was a hot and troublesome evening, and I wanted that night to be different, so I drove after dark to a campsite up on the river, taking a small blue tent, discouraging to the mosquitoes. Although I sort of welcomed the few who were zipping around while I was trying to remember the geometry of the tent. There've been no mosquitoes to speak of in the dry summer. Zip up the tent, lay out a sleeping pad. I've brought a pillow, I'm only a few miles from home.

I used to do this more often, go and sleep in the woods by a river at night. I would do it because it made me pay more attention to my life, despite the fact that I was often easily scared, being alone. I would sleep in the deep ravines of the Red River, in eastern Kentucky, and I would wake at night and listen to the water and imagine I was hearing the voices of children, lost up on the ridges. I remember once leaving at 2:00 A.M., gathering the sleeping bag and pack, clambering up a rocky path by flashlight.

This night, however, is quiet and comfortable. The noise is mostly from tree frogs and a few cicadas. The almost-full moon is a friendly light. A good night for thought, and sleeping.

The poem is by Mary Oliver. It's called *Sleeping in the Forest:*

I thought the earth
remembered me, she
took me back so tenderly, arranging
her dark skirts, her pockets
full of lichens and seeds. I slept
as never before, a stone
on the riverbed, nothing
between me and the white fire of the stars
but my thoughts, and they floated
light as moths among the branches
of the perfect trees. All night
I heard the small kingdoms breathing
around me, the insects, and the birds
who do their work in the darkness. All night
I rose and fell, as if in water, grappling
with a luminous doom. By morning
I had vanished at least a dozen times
into something better.

A bit of rain as the sun came up.

The weather is at last fresh, cool, damp—windy. The breeze blows the white curtains at the window. It is weather to be remarked upon.

"It just could be the best day of the summer."

"Well, that wouldn't be saying much, so far."

We walk in the evening, the last full moon of the summer rising just after eight in the southeast. A few nighthawks ghost about after insects. The nighthawks will soon migrate.

It's South America for the winter. The flowers and the gardens we walk by at dusk now seem fresh, renewed. We've had a week or so of long days with gray skies and rain. The tomatoes especially seem appreciative, and it's their time.

Find an afternoon when it's cool in the kitchen. Gather about a half bushel of plum tomatoes, some onions, some oregano. Wash the glass jars, find the rings and a new box of dome lids, get out the canner. And in the time of a baseball game on the radio, you'll have twenty pints of tomato sauce lined up proudly on the shelf. You've got Thursday night supper almost until next summer.

The best one will be in February, when it's dark at five. You're tired of the cold and wet, and you can pop open the jar of tomato sauce, make spaghetti, and it's summer for a moment. What did it cost? What is it worth?

The grass has returned, needs mowing. I went by a garage sale in town this week and went home with a lawn mower. I was first tempted by a pair of Red Wing work boots for a dollar, but they were a size and a half too big. I resisted the electric wok on the table. Every garage sale has a wok, they are the fondue sets of the eighties. Then, over by the side, there was an old lawn mower. A push mower, four blades, heavy, rusty, a splintered wooden handle. But move it a few feet and it clips the grass nicely, with a sound of precision.

I have a mower at home, but it's newer and tinny compared with this one, not nearly as well made. I talk with the fellow there. "Well," he says, "I need to sell it. I've got no room for it left."

"Well, my wife'll shoot me if I bring home another lawn mower, but it's an interesting one. Would you take six dollars instead of eight?"

"Oh sure, that's fine. Take it on home."

And there it stands in my garage. I cleaned it up some, a Century mower, made in Prophetstown, Illinois. Another label on the handle said, "with Adam's sharpener." But you know, maybe this mower isn't as old as I thought. There is now more time in my memory for things to get old, and surprise me.

My father, one summer in Kentucky, decided to make his own lawn mower, an electric one. We had a big yard and the push mower was exhausting. He used the motor and blade from an old window fan, built a wooden platform with four wheels, and mounted the fan upside down, the blade touching the grass. He hooked a couple of long extension cords together and was off, buzzing across the lawn. The neighbors were amazed. It was the singular mechanical triumph of his life.

At this time of year in Kentucky, late summer in the late 1950s, my life would be football. Two weeks before school started we'd have football practice twice a day. Two hours in the morning; go home, collapse at lunch; then two hours in the afternoon.

The field was dusty, hot. You couldn't take your helmet off, ever. And no water, the coaches believed water made you weak. I guess I knew then why I was doing it.

One year one fellow—Mike—got into an argument with a coach, there was a quick fight, and the next day Mike was in street clothes watching practice. He'd quit the team. And he would stand on the side of the field smoking, drinking a Pepsi, wearing jeans and a T-shirt and a red nylon jacket and boots. This was a time when rebellious teenagers played bongo drums. The coaches warned us we could wind up like him. But he looked pretty good, like James Dean.

I think of those two-a-day practices most often now in winter, when I'm trying to remember what it feels like to be warm and sweaty. I like to have weather experiences to recall; and the other day we went out on the river—just to spend some time in the rain.

Neenah and I tie the canoe on top of the car, and drive north on the Saint Croix and put in. It has been raining for a day or so, and the river is running strong, south. We turn north. The rain, now only a mist, has brought stillness and dripping sounds. Only a few birds trill far back in the woods. We pass some old white pines: tall, isolated memories of a valley once rich in timber, quickly harvested.

In a tree on the Wisconsin side a gray heron leans away from us, away from the danger, and lurches into the air. It drops down a few feet, then levels off near the water with a complaining call, "awk . . . awk." On the Minnesota side a flag flies outside a river cabin, a large flag of Sweden, pale blue with yellow stripes. The trees are soft, indistinct, through the moist air. And for a moment, if your mind blinks, you can sense people on the shore. The past takes color and form.

We go along for about an hour, agree to turn back at the next bend, and there we make a wide turn in the river to face a rainstorm moving north. We put on our jackets. Our legs will just get wet—we're wearing shorts. I take off my glasses and we cruise. The water's moving fast and the paddling is twice as easy, even though we're now heading into the wind.

The rain is the temperature of the river, the temperature of the air. To move from one to the other is not different, and you're breathing air, vapor, water, rain. It is difficult to believe the world has ever been hot and dry. We are enclosed in ourselves, the past and the future as veiled as the valley in mist at summer's end.

## ACKNOWLEDGMENTS

On these pages stand only a few hundred minutes of a year's time. The year, and several months before, made the minutes possible, and that was the work of many friends and colleagues. My thanks to the "Good Evening" staff, our band, the World Theater stagehands and audio and lighting crew, and all the musicians and singers and storytellers and writers and poets and actors and directors who created our programs. My appreciation as well to Minnesota Public Radio, American Public Radio, and especially to our audience—the listeners I could see, and the ones I could trust were there.

Thanks too to the Carpenter Nature Center, and to Jim Gilbert, my first phenologist.

John McPhee's writing has been inspirational in general, and specifically in describing the elements of smoke from a hardwood fire.

Hilary Hinzmann, of W.W. Norton, carefully helped bring these *Notes* from radio to the page. Jonathon Lazear kept telling me it was possible—and jokes. And for smiles and support, I'm grateful to Susan Stamberg, always.